D0623076

THE GAY RIGHTS MOVEMENT

OTHER BOOKS IN THE
AMERICAN SOCIAL MOVEMENTS SERIES:

American Environmentalism
The Animal Rights Movement
The Antinuclear Movement
The Antislavery Movement
The Civil Rights Movement
The Feminist Movement
The Sexual Revolution
The White Separatist Movement

AMERICAN
SOCIAL
MOVEMENTS

THE GAY RIGHTS MOVEMENT

Jennifer Smith, *Book Editor*

Daniel Leone, *President*
Bonnie Szumski, *Publisher*
Scott Barbour, *Managing Editor*

GREENHAVEN
PRESS®

THOMSON
™
GALE

San Diego • Detroit • New York • San Francisco • Cleveland
New Haven, Conn. • Waterville, Maine • London • Munich

THOMSON
★
GALE

LIBRARY OF CONGRESS CATALOGING-IN-PUBLICATION DATA

The gay rights movement / Jennifer Smith, book editor.
   p. cm. — (American social movements)
Includes bibliographical references and index.
ISBN 0-7377-1157-4 (alk. paper) — ISBN 0-7377-1158-2 (lib. : alk. paper)
   1. Gay liberation movement—United States. 2. Gay rights—United States.
I. Smith, Jennifer, 1970– . II. Series.
HQ76.8.U5 G359 2003
305.9'0664'0973—dc21
                                           2002192516

Printed in the United States of America

Contents

Chapter 1 • Origins of the Gay Rights Movement

Chapter 2 • COMING OUT AND COMING TOGETHER

Chapter 3 • THE STRUGGLE FOR SURVIVAL

Chapter 4 • THE GAY COUNTERCULTURE: CONFRONTING CONSERVATISM IN THE MOVEMENT

Chapter 5 • VOICES FROM THE MOVEMENT

FOREWORD

Historians Gary T. Marx and Douglas McAdam define a social movement as "organized efforts to promote or resist change in society that rely, at least in part, on noninstitutionalized forms of political action." Examining American social movements broadens and vitalizes the study of history by allowing students to observe the efforts of ordinary individuals and groups to oppose the established values of their era, often in unconventional ways. The civil rights movement of the twentieth century, for example, began as an effort to challenge legalized racial segregation and garner social and political rights for African Americans. Several grassroots organizations—groups of ordinary citizens committed to social activism—came together to organize boycotts, sit-ins, voter registration drives, and demonstrations to counteract racial discrimination. Initially, the movement faced massive opposition from white citizens, who had long been accustomed to the social standards that required the separation of the races in almost all areas of life. But the movement's consistent use of an innovative form of protest—nonviolent direct action—eventually aroused the public conscience, which in turn paved the way for major legislative victories such as the Civil Rights Act of 1964 and the Voting Rights Act of 1965. Examining the civil rights movement reveals how ordinary people can use nonstandard political strategies to change society.

Investigating the style, tactics, personalities, and ideologies of American social movements also encourages students to learn about aspects of history and culture that may receive scant attention in textbooks. As scholar Eric Foner notes, American history "has been constructed not only in congressional debates and political treatises, but also on plantations and picket lines, in parlors and bedrooms. Frederick Douglass, Eugene V. Debs, and Margaret Sanger . . . are its architects as well as Thomas Jefferson and Abraham Lincoln." While not all

American social movements garner popular support or lead to epoch-changing legislation, they each offer their own unique insight into a young democracy's political dialogue.

Each book in Greenhaven's American Social Movements series allows readers to follow the general progression of a particular social movement—examining its historical roots and beginnings in earlier chapters and relatively recent and contemporary information (or even the movement's demise) in later chapters. With the incorporation of both primary and secondary sources, as well as writings by both supporters and critics of the movement, each anthology provides an engaging panoramic view of its subject. Selections include a variety of readings, such as book excerpts, newspaper articles, speeches, manifestos, literary essays, interviews, and personal narratives. The editors of each volume aim to include the voices of movement leaders and participants as well as the opinions of historians, social analysts, and individuals who have been affected by the movement. This comprehensive approach gives students the opportunity to view these movements both as participants have experienced them and as historians and critics have interpreted them.

Every volume in the American Social Movements series includes an introductory essay that presents a broad historical overview of the movement in question. The annotated table of contents and comprehensive index help readers quickly locate material of interest. Each selection is preceded by an introductory paragraph that summarizes the article's content and provides historical context when necessary. Several other research aids are also present, including brief excerpts of supplementary material, a chronology of major events pertaining to the movement, and an accessible bibliography.

The Greenhaven Press American Social Movements series offers readers an informative introduction to some of the most fascinating groups and ideas in American history. The contents of each anthology provide a valuable resource for general readers as well as for enthusiasts of American political science, history, and culture.

INTRODUCTION

"We still don't even have a name we can all call ourselves. We are many people. We always have been. There is no such thing as a homosexual *anymore, if there ever was. There is no inclusive word to embrace us all.* Gay *is what we're using now, though I know few who are really happy with this word.* Queer *is truly hateful to many, including me. It is a revolting word and a million miles from connoting pride upon its bearers. It took people of color in America many centuries to coalesce as African-Americans. Perhaps we need more time to locate and agree on our name."*[1]

With these words, AIDS activist and author Larry Kramer has captured the disillusionment of many gays and lesbians with the contemporary gay rights movement in the United States. As Marshall Kirk and Hunter Madsen discuss in *After the Ball: How America Will Conquer Its Fear and Hatred of Gays in the '90s,* the belief is that disunity is largely to blame for the movement's lack of political pull on a national scale: "Given the diffuseness of gay power and the chaotic state of gay organization, it's no wonder that our meager advances have come primarily in scattered localities."[2] The movement seems never to have developed beyond a disconnected network of organizations that continue to fight amongst themselves more often than as a united front against discrimination and hatred.

Though the issues have varied throughout the movement's nearly eighty-year history, what has remained is that those fighting over these issues fall into two major factions. The first includes those who see themselves as no different from the rest of society, wanting simply to be treated equally under the law. Detractors of this position within the movement, however, criticize those holding this opinion because they believe it is wrong to assimilate into mainstream society. This second faction rejects the notion that they must think and behave like the majority in society in order to secure their rights. They want to be recognized as different and be acknowledged as having special needs that differ from mainstream society.

THE MOVEMENT BEGINS

Throughout the early years of the United States there was no gay rights movement. Following Henry Gerber, considered the first gay leader, and his short-lived Society for Human Rights (1924), considered the first gay organization, gays and lesbians in the United States did not attempt to publicly organize again until the 1950s. From the start of this second attempt, however, organizers were divided on how best to represent themselves in American society. When Harry Hay founded the first major organization of this era—the Mattachine Foundation in 1950—his intention was to coordinate efforts to change laws that negatively impacted gays, by raising public awareness about homosexuality and fortifying gay culture. Within two years, however, an unfounded accusation by a journalist led to speculation that the organization was a front for Soviet espionage, which sparked public scrutiny of the Mattachines. Though the organization was eventually exonerated of the charge, the newer members demanded patriotic loyalty oaths from all members and a name change to the Mattachine Society, thinking it would distance them from the scandal.

These newer members also insisted upon an image makeover, as noted at the time by activist Jeff Winters:

A proposal was passed to remove the words 'homosexual,' 'ethic,' and 'culture' from the statement of purposes. The reason given was that the words might invite trouble. . . . The public mustn't think that the Society was selfishly interested only in deviates. The policy was accepted that no organized pressure be put on law-makers because it might antagonize them. A person reportedly close to the state legislature insisted that organized pressure never works anyway. And if the homosexual tried to better his lot, the public wouldn't like it at *all*.[3]

This proposal finally drove the founders out and into a rival organization that had sprung to life, fueled by what they perceived as the Mattachine Society's passivity in quashing the denial of gays' and lesbians' basic civil rights.

Following the departure of the Mattachine's founders, ONE, founded in 1952, became the platform for gays who believed that assimilation was both offensive and ineffective. Activist Winters observed in a 1954 issue of *ONE Magazine*, "There are many degrees of both homo- and hetero-sexuality. Actually neither of these words has a valid meaning. To attempt to label everyone either one or the other would require much bigotry or foolishness." Winters, reflecting the less compliant tone of ONE, argued instead that the main reason for gays and lesbians to organize was to secure the basic rights due them as citizens, and because the Mattachine Society was unwilling to do this, a more radical organization must be established: "They must either give over the reins to braver, more capable hands— or stand up and fight. There is no other choice."[4]

Within this time period, a third major gay rights organization emerged. Del Martin and Phyllis Lyon founded the Daughters of Bilitis in 1955, the first lesbian association in the United States. Their intent was not only to offer lesbians a social and discussion group but also to work with other gay organizations toward the common goal of sociopolitical acceptance. However, they too were frustrated by the emergent movement's strategy of assimilation. As Martin notes,

> We suggested [to the gay organizations] that their programs and their publications were not inclusive of or relevant to women. They decried the segregationist organizations which we represented, but would not address themselves to the underlying reasons for the existence of separate women's organizations—that the female homosexual faces sex discrimination not only in the heterosexual world, but within the homophile community.[5]

Because lesbians were seen by society as less threatening than gay men, and their relationships were not forbidden by law, gay organizations embraced them as liaisons to mainstream society, opening doors for discussions with societal and political leaders. Behind closed doors, however, lesbian concerns were often overlooked, and lesbians, as Martin quips, were often relegated to "women's status"—serving coffee and taking notes. In 1970 Martin announced her separation from the movement, marking the beginning of a migration of many lesbians to the burgeoning women's rights movement.

The 1960s and 1970s were times of significant self-reflection and political action, producing both movements for racial equality and women's liberation. Such movements produced other fissures in the growing gay rights movement. Realizing it to be a mainly white, middle-class movement, gays and lesbians of color as well as those living in poverty began to speak out and in some cases break out, forming organizations to focus on their individual concerns. Anita Cornwell, a black lesbian activist during the early 1970s, voiced her frustration and despair in the lesbian journal the *Ladder:*

> Since joining the Movement, I find myself associating mainly with white women. Most of the time I forget there is a racial gap between us, but I sometimes feel that such may not be the case with many of them. That is not a sneaky way of saying racism exists within the Movement—which it does, of course, yet not nearly as much as one would expect considering the nature of our society—but rather that I do miss my black Sisters and yearn for the day when they will embrace the Movement more wholeheartedly. Still, I know why they have not, the main reason being that age-old sickness, racism and sexism, and the damage it has done to us all.[6]

As the 1960s ended, the fractures within the movement finally reached a breaking point, and the frustration and fears of many within the movement erupted in a spontaneous public demonstration.

STONEWALL DEEPENS THE DIVIDE

The Stonewall Inn, a dive bar and disco in New York City, was frequented by drag queens and prostitutes during the latter part of the 1960s. On June 28, 1969, police raided the inn, allegedly for operating without a liquor license, though members of the gay community claimed it was simply harassment. As police made arrests, the inn's patrons fought back. They hurled change and other objects at the police and Molotov cocktails at the bar. The inn was transformed into a staging ground for those who believed that the gay movement had ignored them.

The now infamous Stonewall Inn riots brought a new urgency to the gay rights movement, an urgency that concerned conservative members. As author and professor of religious studies Robert N. Minor declares,

> Was it [the uprising at the Stonewall Inn] led by gay leaders who worried about what straight people would think of them if they didn't remain moderate, middle-of-the-road, "straight-acting," and nice? Of course not. . . . As if to throw the whole issue of LGBT [Lesbian, Gay, Bisexual, and Transgender] classism in our faces, it was led by drag queens and street people. The symbol of our liberation is not the cultured and coiffed but the least understood and the down on their luck, the people looked down upon by others as lazy, dirty, and "low class."[7]

Fueled by the energy of Stonewall, these "low-class" activists founded groups such as the Gay Activists Alliance (GAA), which directly challenged the movement's strategy of assimilation, embodied at the time by the Gay Liberation Front (GLF). The GAA's more confrontational tactics, called zaps, included disrupting political events and forcing their way into the public eye to demand support for their cause. In 1979 Sister Hysterectoria, Sister Secuba, and the Reverend Mother founded the Sisters of Perpetual Indulgence in San Francisco. Part street show, part political action, the Sisters held their first fund-raiser in October of their inaugural year, a bingo/disco benefit for gay Cuban refugees. Though their nuns' habits and "ear brassieres" raised the hackles of moderates everywhere, their benefit performance also raised more than fifteen hundred dollars in that one evening. The Sisters continue to this day with orders in six countries, raising awareness about gay issues with "Sisterly flair."

Although the movement remained fractured through the 1970s, in the following decade common ground would be reached, though not through reconciliation. The specter of AIDS was about to cast its shadow over the gay community.

TRAGEDY BEGETS BRIEF UNITY

When AIDS (autoimmune deficiency syndrome) first gained public attention in the United States in 1981, the gay community had been the hardest hit, yet it was not the only group affected. Intravenous drug users were also contracting the disease. However, because the majority of those dying from AIDS were gay men, the medical journal the *Lancet* called the disease the "gay compromise syndrome," and the *New York Times* called it GRID, or gay-related immune deficiency. These names were seen by many in the movement as bigotry. It was not until the following year, when the disease began to appear in transfusion recipients and hemophiliacs, that public perception about AIDS sufferers began to change.

In this same year, a number of organizations sprang up within the gay rights movement, including the Gay Men's Health Crisis (GMHC), with the goal of raising money for treatments and a cure as well as promoting safe sexual practices in all communities, gay and straight, to halt the spread of the disease. Lesbians and bisexuals from all walks of life fought alongside gay men, and more radical organizations joined as well. The Sisters of Perpetual Indulgence produced safe-sex pamphlets, written by members who were also registered nurses, and raised thousands of dollars. For a time, the movement's separate factions put aside their differences and united against misinformation, discrimination, and the plague that was wiping out their community.

Even in a time of crisis, however, the most united front can crumble. Larry Kramer, a founding member of GMHC, became disillusioned with what he perceived as the GMHC's political passivity. He wanted the group to develop a powerful Washington lobby on par with that of the National Rifle Association:

> I cannot for the life of me understand how the organization I helped to form has become such a bastion of conservatism and such a bureaucratic mess. The bigger you get, the more cowardly you become; the more money you receive, the more self satisfied you are. No longer do you fight for the living; you have become a funeral home. You and your huge assortment of caretakers perform miraculous talks helping the dying to die. I do not cast aspersions on these activities, but I ask you to realize how exceedingly negative this concentration of your energy is. . . . GMHC was founded to utilize any strength it might be fortunate enough to acquire along the way: to bargain with, to fight with, to negotiate with—to use this strength to confront our enemies, to *make* them help us. This is what political strength is all about.[8]

Kramer broke with the GMHC in 1987 and inspired the creation of a more direct action group, ACT UP—the AIDS Coalition to Unleash Power. ACT UP adopted the tactics of such post-Stonewall organizations as the GAA and zapped political figures in an effort to influence the development and release of more effective AIDS treatments. According to Kramer, "Our only salvation lies in aggressive scientific research. This will come only from political pressure."[9]

BECOMING MAINSTREAM

In 1973 the National Gay and Lesbian Task Force (NGLTF) achieved its first victory when the American Psychiatric Association, a group the NGLTF tirelessly pressured, officially ended the status of homosexuality as a mental disease. It also successfully lobbied in 1975 for the first gay rights legislation in Congress and for gays and lesbians to serve in government employment. By 1977 Harvey Milk became the first openly gay elected city official when he won a seat on the San Francisco Board of Supervisors. These ground-breaking achievements opened a door for the movement into the political arena, making activists aware that real change would come not by lobbying alone but, as Milk observed, by also placing gays and lesbians in office.

In the era of AIDS, the major factions within the movement agreed on one important point: they needed to influence those in power. One of the many organizations that sprung to life in the fight against AIDS is the Gay and Lesbian Alliance Against Defamation (GLAAD). Founded in 1985 to protest the *New York Post*'s insensitive and misinformed coverage of the AIDS epidemic, GLAAD grew into a powerful media lobby, educating national outlets as well as Hollywood about more accurate portrayals of gays and lesbians.

Today, gay partnerships and families are no longer hidden but are, in fact, gaining legal recognition. In 1989 Leslea Newman's *Heather Has Two Mommies* and Michael Willhoite's *Daddy's Roommate* were published. In 1996 Hawaii became the first state in the union to recognize gay marriage. Even when the citizens of Hawaii later amended their state constitution to define marriage as a union between one man and one woman, legislators in Vermont refused such an amendment to overturn their Civil Union Law, which was passed in April 2000. This law provides same-sex couples with the same rights, privileges, and responsibilities as heterosexual married couples, including dependent health insurance coverage, hospital visitation, emergency care decisions, estate inheritance, and social security survivor benefits. The rights of gay parents have also been strengthened as sexual orientation has increasingly become less of an issue in many custody and adoption cases.

CHALLENGING THE MAINSTREAM MOVEMENT

Although the gay rights movement has secured several rights and protections, those within the movement believe that complete social acceptance is still a long way off. The schism that remains within the movement itself is evidence of this fact.

Though the movement has made great strides toward embracing all gays and lesbians, exclusion of effeminate men, butch women, bisexuals, and transgenders within the movement continues to be an issue even today. As a bisexual, Rebecca Shuster notes that despite some gains—such as legal recognition—bisexuals still experience discrimination from both the homosexual and heterosexual communities. In addition, transgenders—that is, people who identify with a gender that they were not born with—have yet to secure equal protection under the law. Riki Wilchins, founder of Transexual Menace (a direct-action group) and executive director of GenderPAC (Public Advocacy Coalition), laments the exclusion of gender identity from the political platforms of the mainstream gay rights movement and its Democratic allies. Queer activism is also experiencing a resurgence. *Queer Nasty* is an e-zine (electronic magazine) that provides a voice for those who identify themselves as "queer" and are seen by conservatives within the movement as too evocative of gay stereotypes: "We are tired of being forced to conform to an image of how others think we should be. This includes . . . those in the 'lesbigay' community who think that we are 'harming' them by our actions."[10]

The so-called assimilationist and radical factions that have split the movement since its inception, though united temporarily in the beginning of the AIDS crisis, continue to work against each other. Indeed, it seems as if a centralized national movement may never be a reality due to principle differences: Whereas the "assimilationists" want acceptance to marry, have children, and engage in politics or the military just as others do, "radicals" see these mainstream institutions as symbols of their oppression not worthy of their allegiance; they simply want the freedom to live life as they choose.

Echoing the same disenchantment as is reflected in the quote from Kramer that began this essay, Mark Blasius and Shane Phelan, editors of *We Are Everywhere: A Historical Sourcebook of Gay and Lesbian Politics* ask, "Can we speak of 'the lesbian and gay movement,' or only of several movements by lesbians and gays collaborating for expedience in the achievement of particular political ends? To what extent are we fighting for the same things, and to what extent are our agendas divergent or opposed?"[11]

Despite this internal dissension, the American gay rights movement has gained both social and legal victories over the past eighty years in the fight to secure equal rights for gay, lesbian, bisexual, and transgender Americans. This anthology examines the movement in more detail and introduces both key figures and issues.

NOTES

1. Larry Kramer, "Yesterday, Today, and Tomorrow," *Advocate*, March 1999. www.advocate.com.

2. Marshall Kirk and Hunter Madsen, *After the Ball: How America Will Conquer Its Fear and Hatred of Gays in the '90s.* New York: Doubleday, 1989.

3. Jeff Winters, "A Frank Look at the Mattachine: Can Homosexuals Organize?" *ONE Magazine*, 1954.

4. Winters, "A Frank Look at the Mattachine."

5. Del Martin, "If That's All There Is," *Ladder*, 1970.

6. Anita Cornwell, "From a Soul Sister's Notebook," *Ladder*, 1972.

7. Robert N. Minor, "The Legend of the Stonewall Inn: What Does It Mean?" *Gay Today*, June 17, 2002. http://gaytoday.badpuppy.com.

8. Larry Kramer, *Reports from the Holocaust: The Making of an AIDS Activist.* New York: St. Martin's, 1989.

9. Kramer, *Reports from the Holocaust.*

10. *Queer Nasty*, January 31, 2002. www.tripnet.com.

11. Mark Blasius and Shane Phelan, eds., *We Are Everywhere: A Historical Sourcebook of Gay and Lesbian Politics.* New York: Routledge, 1997.

CHAPTER 1

ORIGINS OF THE GAY RIGHTS MOVEMENT

AMERICAN
SOCIAL
MOVEMENTS

Homosexuality Is Not a Disease

HENRY GERBER (UNDER THE PSEUDONYM PARISEX)

Thought of as the first gay leader in the United States, Henry Gerber served from 1920 to 1923 with the U.S. Army of Occupation in Germany, where he became involved in the German gay rights movement. Upon returning home, Gerber sought to organize Chicago's gay residents and set in motion an American gay rights movement. The Society for Human Rights (SHR) came into being in December 1924, and began publication of its journal, *Friendship and Freedom*. In July 1925, a member's wife complained to the police after she discovered her husband's secret; the police arrested all SHR members—simply being gay was a crime back then—and shut the society down. Gerber survived three trials—a judge finally ruled in his favor because the police never had a search warrant—but lost his job with the postal service.

Gerber left Chicago, re-enlisted in the army, and served seventeen more years before retiring. He was able to continue his activism, however, by quietly supporting both the Mattachine Society and ONE—the first two major gay organizations founded in the 1950s—and writing in the gay press under a pseudonym, Parisex. It is under this identity that Gerber wrote the following response to "The Riddle of Homosexuality" by Dr. W. Béran Wolfe, who claimed that homosexuality—or "inversion" as he referred to it— was a mental disorder that could be "cured." Gerber's impassioned defense of gay rights struck a chord with the gay community and has inspired more than one generation of gay rights activists.

After reading the article ["The Riddle of Homosexuality"] by W. Béran Wolfe, M.D., in the April [1932] issue of

The Modern Thinker, one cannot but deeply sympathize with the inverts for being the world's eternal scapegoats. In the early Middle Ages the Papacy stipulated that "sodomers, heretics and sorcerers be burned." When the legal control of the population slipped from the hands of Mother Church into that of the legislatures and politicians, better times came for the homosexuals in that their sexual "crimes" were considered less heinous. After Napoleon had written his liberal code, homosexuals were no longer molested by the law in Latin countries, but in the Anglo-Saxon world, in England and the United States, persecution of them is still in vogue, and as recently as the year 1915 the legislature of the State of California passed a new law, extending the scope of the term of sodomy. Today a more lenient attitude is being shown to homosexuals by the law. On October 16, 1929, the German committee of the Reichstag [Parliament], discussing the new German legal code, proposed to abolish punishment for homosexual acts *per se,* between *men,* and in Russia, of course, the medieval persecution of homosexuals was repudiated with religious superstitions.

Now, that the inverts have almost escaped the stake and the prison, the psychoanalysts threaten them with the new danger of the psychiatric torture chamber. It is not to be wondered that a priest, a legislator and a psychoanalyst should be interested only in their dogmas. The priest is as much convinced of his sin theory as the legislator is sure that prison is the cure of crime, and the psychoanalyst, not a bit less, is certain that his therapy will bring back the erring homosexual to the normal fold. But he is strangely silent on the method.

Of course, the chief fallacy of psychiatry and similar trades is that it puts the cart before the horse. If we may believe the psychoanalysts, it is not modern machine civilization, at great variance with nature, that is conducive to neuroses, but civilization itself is the norm, and anything else, even nature, is perverse and neurotic. Nature, which has struggled along valiantly these million years, is now being told by the Freuds, the Adlers, the Jungs, and their slavish followers, that its manifold sex urges are abnormal, and that civilization, that recent upstart, is the only norm of life; that if one reverted to good old mother nature he would quickly be accused of no less a crime than seeking to flee from reality. As if it needed homosexuality, impotence and other "neuroses" nowadays to drive a man crazy! Are not the long lines of unemployed, the starving, those cheated out of their lives' savings by the leaders of society and those married and unable to feed their brood, enough reasons for mental, physical and moral breakdowns?

And what about the homosexual fleeing from reality? Thousands of priests, nuns, monks, choose celibacy to avoid "normal sex life." Psychoanalysts undoubtedly include them too in their long list of "neurotics"; still there is no law compelling anyone to marry. As to social responsibilities of homosexuals, I am not aware of their having been exempted in the late war, neither do I see on the tax blanks where the unmarried homosexuals pay less than the heterosexual who is not fleeing from reality; nor do I know of any place of employment where the homosexual is not required to work as hard for his pennies as the heterosexual worker. Is it perhaps an exception to the psychoanalyst's rule of neurotic symptoms for those avoiding "normal sex life" that the psychoanalytic studios are filled with married women but shunned by the "neurotic" homosexuals?

DISCRIMINATION, NOT LIFESTYLE, CREATES NEUROSES

And is not the psychiatrist again putting the cart before the horse in saying that homosexuality is a symptom of a neurotic style of life? Would it not sound more natural to say that the homosexual is made neurotic because his style of life is beset by thousands of dangers? What heterosexual would not turn highly neurotic were his mode of love marked "criminal," and were he liable to be pulled into prison every time he wanted to satisfy his sex urge—not to speak of the dangers of being at all times exposed to blackmail by heterosexuals who prey upon him, and the ostracism of society? Were he not clever in pretending to be "normal," he would lose his place of employment quickly. This constant insecurity and danger from all sides would drive anyone into any number of neuroses. That the average homosexual even in spite of a thousand dangers does not want to be "cured" and wants nothing but to be left alone by hypocritical meddlers, and feels comparatively happy in his love, is evidence enough that his condition cannot be merely acquired.

If it were so easy to "cure" a homosexual, the homosexuals would flock to the psychiatrists, and instead of having to ask the authorities to establish free clinics for homosexuals, the landscape would be dotted with such hospitals. The surgeon removing the "queer" complex would find his practice as profitable as that of taking out tonsils and appendices. While Dr. Wolfe unhesitatingly affirms the question whether homosexuality can be cured, how, where, and for how much this can be done, the deponent sayeth not. I doubt if there ever was a cure of a genuine homosexual. Such cures have been reported once and then, but they are as temporary as the famous experiments of Dr. [Eugen] Steinach and the monkey gland transplantations [to cure homosexuality]. It stands to reason that a homosexual cannot be cured (and the doctor cautiously adds: provided the homosexual *wants* to be cured) because if he showed any interest in women he would simply not be a homosexual. The few cures reported were brought about by alleged heterosexual suggestions to the "patient," but [Magnus] Hirschfeld points out very clearly the absurdity of suggesting to a homosexual to get married. There are thousands of homosexuals who are married, upon the advice of doctors, and unless they were strongly bisexually inclined, not even marriage has cured them. The homosexual man does not shun women because he wants to flee from the reality of normal sex life, but because he himself is physically a woman and his normal sex life is directed to the other sex, another man, the only person to attract him. According to the physical formula, opposite poles attract each other, while like poles repel each other.

It is highly improbable that an intelligent homosexual could be "cured" by suggesting to him the blessings of monogamy, an institution which, according to Russell, Calverton, Schmalhausen, Lindsey and other modern writers resembles a ship full of leaks, ready to sink at any moment. Few homosexuals are stupid enough to forget the scandalous divorce courts, the ever increasing desertions, and marital unhappiness in general, to decide to jump from the frying pan into the fire. Too much pessimism, of course, is uncalled for, but anyone acquainted with the real life of homosexuals or heterosexuals will have to admit that many heterosexuals lead a happy life, but also that homosexuals live in happy, blissful unions, especially in Europe, where homosexuals are unmolested as long as they mind their own business, and are not, as in England and in the United States, driven to the underworld of perversions and crime for satisfaction of their very real craving for love.

Nowadays, when commissioners of health and other medical authorities sell their names to advertise the gadgets of clever business concerns, one would not find it so much out of place, if (presumed Dr. Wolfe were broadcasting his article on homosexuality) the radio announcer would after the closing words of the good doctor enunciate: This program comes to you through the courtesy of John Doe, manufacturer of baby carriages. As a matter of fact, one finds the law against invert sex acts and other sex taboos labeled in some state penal codes as: *Laws for the Protection of the Christian Institution of Marriage.*

CONTRADICTIONS IN THE OPPOSING VIEWPOINT

But the contradictions in his article alone disprove the various statements of Dr. Wolfe. Let me point out only the most glaring ones. He says on page 99: "Analytic investigation of the invert's total personality demonstrates *practically without exception* a basic misanthropy of the invert." On page 96 he says: "Today homosexual 'joints', homosexual 'drags', homosexual plays, and homosexual clubs are known in every large American city," and again on page 99: "Homosexuality is unique in that the homosexual neurotics form communities and thus develop a certain social feeling." They are then not misanthropes without exception, but rather as gregarious as the heterosexuals who also may be found congregating in ball rooms, clubs and "joints." One cannot really blame the parisexual [homosexual] if he is not very much in love with heterosexuals who exploit and persecute him and make his life miserable.

The fact that scientific information concerning the nature of homosexuality is almost unobtainable is not due to the ignorance of the medical profession but to the public policy of suppressing anything truthful about homosexuals. The truth about homosexuals is suppressed in the same degree as the knowledge of birth control, for homosexuality, of course, is but one of the many natural forms of birth control.

It is ridiculous to assume that the whole Greek nation was neurotic because homosexuality was practiced there with the sanction of the state. Homosexuality even exists among the primitive tribes and among animals, though this fact also has been suppressed. It must be more than a neurosis if a certain natural trait persists throughout all ages and still carries on after the most cruel and fatal persecution of those so inclined. It is not very clear how one could "easily" escape the reality of normal sex life by merely adopting a sex mode the very practice of which is punished with penitentiary terms, with social ruin and the danger of blackmail from all directions. But many heterosexuals are also in jails, socially ruined by jealous competitors and blackmailed by greedy women. It is so much easier to conform to conventionality and marry. The politicians have always believed that they could put over their various panaceas to make the world perfect according to their beliefs. They have sponsored their sacred institution of monogamy by propaganda in all fields of public education, and not enough with this, have surrounded holy wedlock with vicious taboos, punishing the violators with penitentiary terms; they have passed the 18th Amendment to stop people from drinking [repealed in 1933 by the Twenty-First Amendment], but we see in reality only about 50% of the population married, and getting plenty of booze to drink. One cannot enforce a law against natural cravings. Taboos always result in bootleggers of love or drink. The very fact that it takes so many laws to enforce monogamy at once labels it only an ideal but not a natural institution. One never hears of laws compelling people to eat! Sex and drink are very closely related. Where sex laws are lenient, as in Latin countries, people drink more modestly, but the Protestant countries are notorious for hard drinking and drunkenness. Drinking is another "neurosis," an effort to escape the bitter reality of the "responsibilities of normal sex life." But intoxication is not *per se* punished.

The Bible story on which the persecution of the homosexuals is based even now, is also full of contradictions, for it tells of the willingness of Yahwe to save the wicked city if there were only five righteous among the citizens (that is, those not given to sodomy). But not even five could be found. The men and women, both young and old (*Genesis:* all the people from every quarter), surrounded Lot. One wonders by which methods the children of the homosexuals were produced!

WHAT IS "NORMAL"?

Dr. Wolfe states that a too great desire for complete security characterizes all inverts. Page the premier of France! 50,000,000 cannot be neurotic! In these days of insecurity, general unemployment and racketeering, one does not need to be a homosexual to feel the need for more security in employment, house and home. All the other symptoms of neurosis which the doctor here enumerates are too general to be blamed merely upon homosexuals. The inferiority complex? We wonder how many people in very high ranks of life are homosexual without being suspected? And they might be considered the very acmes of superiority and excellent character. [Arthur] Schopenhauer said that those who look for the devil with horns and claws and clanging bells are always fooled. Conventional opinion looks for homosexuals only in the gutters. It is not fair to hold up a homosexual in the gutter to the scorn of the normal world and maintain that all homosexuals practically without an exception are like him. Heterosexuals do not point to their weakest member for the benefit of the homosexuals. There are hundreds of homosexuals among the pillars of society and no one knows of their being homosexual, except perhaps a cute little boy prostitute in Paris.

We cannot all be bank presidents and millionaires, but the percentage of homosexuals among the lowly workers is not greater than that of the number of heterosexuals. Homosexuals often occupy well-paid positions as secretaries and bank clerks and not rarely hold positions of trust. Especially in hospitals they are considered more valuable than heterosexual men.

The writer knows several elderly homosexuals of wealth

Sigmund Freud Comments on a Homosexual Cure

By asking me if I can help, you mean, I suppose, if I can abolish homosexuality and make normal heterosexuality take its place. The answer is, in a general way, we cannot promise to achieve it. In a certain number of cases we succeed in developing the blighted germs of heterosexual tendencies which are present in every homosexual, [but] in the majority of cases it is no more possible. It is a question of the quality and the age of the individual. The result of the treatment cannot be predicted.

What analysis can do for your son runs in a different line. If he is unhappy, neurotic, torn by conflicts, inhibited in his social life, analysis may bring him harmony, peace of mind, full efficiency, whether he remains a homosexual or gets changed.

"Letter to an American Mother," *American Journal of Psychiatry*, vol. 107, 1951, p. 787. Found online at *People with a History*. Ed. Paul Halsall. www.fordham.edu/halsall/pwh/freud1.html.

who spend part of their incomes for the support of unfortunate children deserted by their parents and interned in orphan asylums.

If homosexuals were stupid enough openly to make converts to their aberrations they would not be at liberty very long, for the public policy demands a stern suppression of homosexuality.

"Homosexuality often becomes criminal because of their aggressive acts against society," says Dr. Wolfe. It would be interesting to look up the statistical figures of crimes. Thus it might surprise Dr. Wolfe that the average annual convictions for sodomy in the State of New York are only about 15, while the number of cases of rape, adultery, and other sexual delinquencies of heterosexuals reaches many hundred cases. It must be remembered also that the sodomy law in the State of New York likewise punishes heterosexual men and women convicted of committing certain sexual perversions. The statement of Dr. Wolfe that homosexual sex acts are a penitentiary offence is not a fact. There are certain extreme sex acts which are punished by law, but it makes no difference at all whether the perpetrators are homosexuals or heterosexuals. Many homosexual sex acts are not punished at all, neither is homosexuality *per se*. The inability of our legislators properly to evaluate social phenomena is significant. While two grown-up persons who in private with mutual agreement perform a certain harmless sex act, may be sent to prison for twenty years (or life as in the State of Georgia), a syphilitic may freely spread his loathsome disease to wife and children without the law lifting a finger. Our sex laws are still based on the ignorance of Christian sex morality.

PREJUDICED PROPAGANDA

While we must congratulate Dr. Wolfe on his courageous stand in the matter of punishing homosexuals, we do not believe that homosexuals would want to be freed from the jails in turn to be put in lunatic asylums. But, no doubt, there are many psychologists looking for jobs and they are as desirous of getting onto the public payrolls as other vendors of nostrums [questionable remedies].

If homosexuals were permitted to let loose one-tenth as much propaganda about homosexuality as the heterosexuals (the stage, radio, film, literature, theatre, and especially the vaudeville, reek with a nauseating display of female legs and whatnot—while homosexual propaganda is entirely out of question) we wonder if there would not be much more homosexual "neuroses" present. Even today the works of Havelock Ellis on sex are banned from the mails because he does not moralize on inversion. It is well known that a great number of homosexuals are only attracted by masculine men of normal inclinations, and if they tried to convert all men to homosexuality, they would defeat their own purpose.

To make an analogy of homosexuality with epilepsy is highly arbitrary insofar as Dr. Wolfe himself has stated in his article (page 99) that homosexuality is not a disease in itself. It is, of course, just as ridiculous to state that homosexuals have a greater number of truly great men among their ranks as it would be to maintain that a man could not be a genius because of his being homosexual. Many inverts are driven to introversion by the hostile attitude of society and thus often turn to study and literature instead of watching ball games, prize fights and other pastimes of the heterosexuals.

After considering Dr. Wolfe's thesis one is somewhat in doubt whether he is interested in homosexuality or whether he is interested in squaring it with the Adlerian individual psychology [which seeks a balance between one's needs and social responsibility], of which he is so obviously an advocate. It must seem to a layman intelligence that the latter case is the true one. There is a matter of finality about his findings and his "remedy" that, to the body of scientists who realize the complexity of this field and who admit that they are only at the beginning of the solution, must appear engagingly naïve. One is suspicious of anyone who approaches an intricate phase of life with a definite theory, for the simple reason that he is apt to find something that will not tally with his original theoretical pre-possessions, and his pride of theory is very apt to prevent him from sacrificing the theory.

NATURE OR NURTURE—OR BOTH?

Once more we are told that inversion is not a matter of biology or physiology, but is acquired by social conditions and determined by "early childhood experiences." We are shown the proof of this by the statement that homosexuals as children, "in the vast majority" of cases, occupy an ordinal position in the family—that is, they are almost always the oldest or youngest child, that also the father dies early (in the boy's case) and that the resulting coddling of the boy by its mother ultimately makes the boy homosexual. Suppose this is true: How then will psychiatric therapy of the "individual homosexual" effect a cure? Supposing such a cure possible, supposing further that each homosexual could be prevailed upon to submit to this cure (which is preposterous) the fact would still remain that in every generation there would be another crop of homosexuals, simply because boys still continued to be first and last children, losing their fathers and mothers early in life. If it is true that the "ordinal family position" occupied by the incipient homosexual is a basic cause of homosexuality, how can curing the individual results of such family conditions abolish the root of the condition? According to this view the only possible way to exterminate homosexuality is to alter social conditions, to see that no married couple has a first or a last child, and that neither the father nor mother die while the child is yet young.

The making of the homosexual, we are further assured, does not, however, cease in the family conditions. Increasing maturity intensifies his difficulties. Still more hellish is the fact that segregation of the sexes aggravates the situation. Segregation in schools—and, it might be added, the army, navy, labor and prison camps; this may be true, somewhat, but how will individual therapy solve it? By arranging society so that no army, navy, prison and labor camps and schools will be necessary, it would seem.

Next he introduces the factor of masturbation as a formative element in the making of homosexuality. The idea seems to be that masturbation is peculiar to homosexuals. But every heterosexual who reads that passage will know that this is absurdly false. Havelock Ellis shows that 60% of theological students practice it. Dr. Max Huhner says that any man who denies it is a liar. There can be no actual statistics about the extent of masturbation, but McCabe states that most of the estimates given vary between 90 and 99% of the adult community. Thus, were the practice of masturbation an indication of homosexuality, we would find 95% of the population homosexual rather than an alleged 5%.

RECOGNIZING OUR SOCIAL VALUE

That social conditions, environment, may be a factor in homosexuality is no doubt true, but it is not *the* factor. Is character, anyone's character, a matter of physical constitution, or is it a product of environment? It seems absurd to stress one of those factors. Both are necessary, and it is yet impossible to say which is the more important and formative. They both act on and supplement each other. A good seed planted in poor soil will result in little. A poor seed planted in the richest soil will similarly result in little. Who can say at what point physical structure ends and environment begins? Who can say whether the excellence of a fruit is due to the inherent qualities of the seed, or the qualities of the soil that nourished it? Dr. Wolfe says it is all a matter of soil.

He is so intent on improving the mental health of society by condemning the homosexual, so busy listing the evil and vicious aspects of inversion, that he nowhere asks the question: Is it possible that homosexuality, in the final analysis, does contribute something of value to society? Yes, he points out that though [Oscar] Wilde, [Leonardo] da Vinci, and others (to name but a few) were homosexuals, "this is hardly a valid argument for being homosexual." As though becoming a homosexual were a matter of choice! He fails to account for those homosexual geniuses, and takes arbitrary refuge in holding up to scorn and contempt the prostitutes, the "seducers," making it appear further that these boy prostitutes are innocent victims. This thin trick should fool nobody. Prostitution is a large and perpetual element in heterosexuality, and no doubt many people believe that heterosexual women prostitutes are seduced into their profession, which leaves room for much doubt. A large per cent of girl prostitutes are so by choice, nothing else. And while social conditions are such that prostitution must be even more closely associated with homosexuality, homosexuality offers therefore opportunities of exploitation through blackmail, etc., that are not possible to such a large extent among heterosexual prostitutes. But such argument by Dr. Wolfe is arbitrary. Would he cast any such reflection on heterosexual great men by some one who detracted from their greatness by pointing out the heterosexual seducers and prostitutes? Arbitrary indeed.

He does not ask anywhere whether homosexuality might not have a social value. On the face of it, there must be some social gain in homosexuality. Homosexuality has existed from the beginning of time, in all sorts of social regimes and conditions. It is a *constant* human quality. It survives, almost if at all, undiminished since the dawn of history. Why? There has to be a reason somewhere, and that reason must be one of utility, of human value, else it could not survive. If the homosexuality of geniuses does not prove that homosexuality is a higher order, it certainly does prove that homosexuality is not exclusively an affliction of gutter snipes, maniacs, and thugs. Can anyone say definitely that homosexuality has not in the past contributed valuable things to society—unsuspected things perhaps—or that homosexuality, by its strange duality of character, may not fill an important function in the future of society?

Dr. Wolfe is at pains to list the defects and weaknesses of the homosexual temperament, but none of the fine and worthy qualities: the artistic nature of the homosexual man, his sensitive spirit, his rhythmic emotions, his "hardihood of intellect and body," or his capacities for friendship. I find myself in sympathy with the statement of Edward Carpenter, in his intelligent and human book, *Love's Coming of Age:* "It may be said to give them both (women and men of homosexual inclination) through their double nature, command of life in all its phases, and a certain free-masonry of the secrets of the two sexes which may well favor their function as reconcilers and interpreters." There are the great artists of the world, wholly or partially homosexual, Michaelangelo, Shakespeare, Alexander, Julius Caesar, Christine, Sappho, and the rest. Whether or not homosexuality has been a large factor in genius, it has been closely associated with it, and that significant fact has not yet been explained away. And further, who will say that an element of homosexuality is not today woven into the temperament of our artists and creators and interpreters? And that it will not continue to be in the future? The extermination of homosexuality, even if it were possible, might result in a very jagged hole in the fabric of society and its culture; might, in fact, be a costly experiment.

NATURE IS NOT PERVERSE—CIVILIZATION IS

But there is a yet more complex problem attached to this therapeutic cure of homosexuality. Dr. Wolfe gives the impression that homosexuality centers around actual sexual intercourse, that it is exclusively absorbed with intercourse and the act itself. But there are all shades and degrees of homosexuality, from Platonic, spiritual attachments down to the sexual. Where is the psychiatrist to draw the line here? Will he cure the homosexual who is literally sexual, and permit to exist all the varying shades of attachment between similar sexes, attachments that verge close to the sexual border and are yet beyond it? There is no hard and fast distinction between friendship and love—friendship can and does deepen into love. Therapeutic methods, developed to their ultimate capacities, would, it seems, cast suspicion on friendships existing between members of the same sex, however non-homosexual those friendships might really be. Such a state of affairs might inconvenience many people, including heterosexuals; including also Dr. Wolfe, of course.

While Dr. Wolfe upbraids the apologists of homosexuality as liable to forget the far greater number of dilapidated homosexuals who are brought into police courts, he is strangely silent on the fact that normal heterosexuals also clutter up police stations. And why harp on the very few homosexuals who find satisfaction for their pathological craving to deal with the young boys, when the papers are at present full of the details of atrocious killings of little girls by mentally deranged heterosexual men? The cinemas in which homosexuals often seek contact with their kind are closed to minors, and the homosexuals who prefer the very young boys are as rare as the heterosexual "cradle snatchers." These shows are full of heterosexual prostitutes who as rugged individualists have long ago caught up with the ready market for young men, and they, like their heterosexual sisters of the street, are not as innocent as Dr. Wolfe might think. The youth of 16 or 17 is no longer ignorant of masturbation and other onanistic [self-gratifying] acts, and to blame the seduction of all boys on the homosexuals is a bit exaggerated. There is much work for the police to save the youth of today from heterosexual seduction and venereal infection, and the pot should not call the kettle black.

One who knows the world and life will not have to look far for "neurotic" camouflage to find the motive of the average young bachelor who is not willing to take up the "normal" mode of sex life, i.e. monogamy. In a society where monogamy is a contract in many ways disadvantageous to men and which is on all sides admitted to be a tottering institution, one need not accuse the hard-beset man of trying to "flee from reality." He is merely wisely avoiding trouble. There are too many plain reasons for his preferring to remain single to need dragging the red herring of neurosis across the road. Are all the men in the army and navy, who constitute the first line of defense of our nation, and who are unable to find "normal sex life" with its social obligations, therefore neurotics?

If the theory of [Otto] Weininger is faulty, so is the theory of [Arthur] Adler, for while there are admittedly a great number of neurotics among the homosexuals, whose lives are made miserable by heterosexual persecution, there are also a great number of homosexuals who go through life every bit as "normal", healthy, and morally of value to society. The theory of Adler plainly does not fit here. Dr. Hirschfeld has examined thousands of homosexuals and his reports do not bring out the general theory of Dr. Adler and of psychoanalysis, which science Dr. [Otto] Jastrow calls the "most amazing vagary in the history of Twentieth Century thought." Even psychoanalysts do not agree among themselves as to the cause of homosexuality. Dr. Wilhelm Stekel, while he also holds to the neurosis theory, at least admits that a person is by nature, normally, bisexual, and that a person who represses his heterosexuality is just as neurotic as a homosexual who represses or attempts to repress his sexual part of nature.

After all, it is highly futile for Dr. Wolfe to worry about neurotic homosexuals when the world itself, led and ruled by the strong heterosexual "normal" men is in such chaotic condition, and knows not where to turn.

It is quite possible that if called upon, the homosexuals in this country would put up the money to send Dr. Wolfe to Washington to examine these great big "normal" men, who guide the destinies of millions, to find their "neurosis" and to cure it.

The Homosexual Is Part of Nature's Complexity

JAMES BALDWIN

James Baldwin, the literary giant born in Harlem in 1924, became so disillusioned by race relations in the United States that he moved to Paris in 1948. While there, he wrote one of his most important works, *Go Tell It on the Mountain*, a partially autobiographical look at his youth. In the 1960s, Baldwin began to alternate between Paris and New York. He also became politically active in the American civil rights movement, both as a black man and a gay man.

The following essay, published in 1949, explores the depiction of homosexuality in society and literature. Baldwin argues that stereotypical depictions of macho men and cowering or conniving women infantilize society's understanding of relations between men and women by assigning such predetermined descriptions to male and female roles. Only when we end such stereotyping—a trend, Baldwin implies, which literature can help set—will society move beyond heterosexual and homosexual toward acceptance.

The problem of the homosexual, so vociferously involved with good and evil, the unnatural as opposed to the natural, has its roots in the nature of man and woman and their relationship to one another. While at one time we speak of nature and at another of the nature of man, we speak on both occasions of something of which we know very little and we make the tacit admission that they are not one and the same. Between nature and man there is a difference; there is, indeed, perpetual war. It develops when we think about it that not

James Baldwin, "Preservation of Innocence," *Zero*, vol. 1, Summer 1949, pp. 14–22. Copyright © 1949 by The Zero Press. Reproduced by permission.

only is a natural state perversely indefinable outside of the womb or before the grave but that it is not on the whole a state which is altogether desirable. It is just as well that we cook our food and are not baffled by water-closets and do not copulate in the public thoroughfare. People who have not learned this are not admired as natural but are feared as primitive or incarcerated as insane. We spend vast amounts of our time and emotional energy in learning how not to be natural and in eluding the trap of our own nature and it therefore becomes very difficult to know exactly what is meant when we speak of the unnatural. It is not possible to have it both ways, to use nature at one time as the final arbiter of human conduct and at another to oppose her as angrily as we do. As we are being inaccurate, perhaps desperately defensive and making, inversely, a most damaging admission when we describe as inhuman some reprehensible act committed by a human being, so we become hopelessly involved in paradox when we describe as unnatural something which is found in nature. A cat torturing a mouse to death is not described as inhuman for we assume that it is being perfectly natural; nor is a table condemned as being unnatural for we know that it has nothing to do with nature. What we really seem to be saying when we speak of the inhuman is that we cannot bear to be confronted with that fathomless baseness shared by all humanity and when we speak of the unnatural that we cannot imagine what vexations nature will dream up next. We have, in short, whenever nature is invoked to support our human divisions, every right to be suspicious, nature having betrayed only the most perplexing and untrustworthy interest in man and none whatever in his institutions. We resent this indifference and we are frightened by it; we resist it; we ceaselessly assert the miracle of our existence against this implacable power. Yet we know nothing of birth or death except that we remain powerless when faced by either. Much as we resent or threaten or cajole nature she refuses absolutely to relent; she may at any moment throw down the trump card she never fails to have hidden and leave us bankrupt. In time, her ally and her rather too explicit witness, suns rise and set and the face of the earth changes; at length the limbs stiffen and the light goes out of the eyes.

> *And nothing 'gainst time's scythe may make defense*
> *Save breed to brave him when he takes thee hence.*

We arrive at the oldest, the most insistent and the most vehement charge faced by the homosexual: he is unnatural because he has turned from his life-giving function to a union which is sterile. This may, in itself, be considered a heavy, even an unforgivable crime, but since it is not so considered when involving other people, the unmarried or the poverty-stricken or the feeble, and since his existence did not always invoke that hysteria with which he now contends, we are safe in suggesting that his present untouchability owes its motive power to several other sources. Let me suggest that his present debasement and our obsession with him corresponds to the debasement of the relationship between the sexes; and that his ambiguous and terrible position in our society reflects the ambiguities and terrors which time has deposited on that relationship as the sea piles seaweed and wreckage along the shore.

For, after all, I take it that no one can be seriously disturbed about the birth-rate: when the race commits suicide it will not be in Sodom. Nor can we continue to shout unnatural whenever we are confronted by a phenomenon as old as mankind, a phenomenon, moreover, which nature has maliciously repeated in all of her domain. If we are going to be natural then this is part of nature; if we refuse to accept this, then we have rejected nature and must find another criterion.

ACCEPTING THE COMPLEXITY OF HUMAN NATURE

Instantly the Deity springs to mind, in much the same manner, I suspect, that he sprang into being on the cold, black day when we discovered that nature cared nothing for us. His advent, which alone had the power to save us from nature and ourselves, also created a self-awareness and, therefore, tensions and terrors and responsibilities with which we had not coped before. It marked the death of innocence; it set up the duality of good-and-evil; and now Sin and Redemption, those mighty bells, began that crying which will not cease until, by another act of creation, we transcend our old morality. Before we were banished from Eden and the curse was uttered, «I will put enmity between thee and the woman», the homosexual did not exist; nor, properly speaking, did the heterosexual. We were all in a state of nature.

We are forced to consider this tension between God and nature and are thus confronted with the nature of God because He is man's most intense creation and it is not in the sight of nature that the homosexual is condemned, but in the sight of God. This argues a profound and dangerous failure of concept, since an incalculable number of the world's humans are thereby condemned to something less than life; and we may not, of course, do this without limiting ourselves. Life, it is true, is a process of decisions and alternatives, the conscious awareness and acceptance of limitations. Experience, nevertheless, to say nothing of history, seems clearly to indicate that it is not possible to banish or to falsify any human need without ourselves undergoing falsification and loss. And what of murder? A human characteristic, surely. Must we embrace the murderer? But the question must be put another way: is it possible not to embrace him? For he is in us and of us. We may not be free until we understand him.

The nature of man and woman and their relationship to one another fills seas of conjecture and an immense proportion of the myth, legend and literature of the world is devoted to this subject. It has caused, we gather, on the evidence presented by any library, no little discomfort. It is observable that the more we imagine we have discovered the less we know and that, moreover, the necessity to discover and the effort and self-consciousness involved in this necessity makes this relationship more and more complex. Men and women seem to function as imperfect and sometimes unwilling mirrors for one another; a falsification or distortion of the nature of the one is immediately reflected in the nature of the other. A division between them can only betray a division within the soul of each. Matters are not helped if we thereupon decide that men must recapture their status as men and that women must embrace their function as women; not only does the resulting rigidity of attitude put to death any possible communion, but, having once listed the bald physical facts, no one is prepared to go further and decide, of our multiple human attributes, which are masculine and which are feminine. Directly we say that women have finer and more delicate sensibilities we are reminded that she is insistently, mythically and even historically, treacherous. If we are so rash as to say that men have greater endurance, we are reminded of the procession of men who have gone to their long home while women walked about the streets—mourning, we are told, but no doubt, gossiping and shopping at the same time. We can pick up no novel, no drama, no poem; we may examine no fable nor any myth without stumbling on this merciless paradox in the nature of the sexes. This is a paradox which experience alone is able to illuminate and this experience is not communicable in any language that we know. The recognition of this complexity is the signal of maturity; it marks the death of the child and the birth of the man.

LITERATURE PERPETUATES STEREOTYPES

One may say, with an exaggeration vastly more apparent than real, that it is one of the major American ambitions to shun this metamorphosis. In the truly awesome attempt of the American to at once preserve his innocence and arrive at a man's estate, that mindless monster, the tough guy, has been created and perfected; whose masculinity is found in the most infantile and elementary externals and whose attitude towards women is the wedding of the most abysmal romanticism and the most implacable distrust. It is impossible for a moment to believe that any James M. Cain or Raymond Chandler hero loves his girl; we are given overwhelming evidence that he wants her, but that is not the same thing and, moreover, what he seems to want is revenge; what they bring to each other is not even passion or sexuality but an unbelievably barren and wrathful grinding. They are surrounded by blood and treachery; and their bitter coupling, which has the urgency and precision of machine-gun fire, is heralded and punctuated by the mysterious and astounded corpse. The woman, in these energetic works, is the unknown quantity, the incarnation of sexual evil, the smiler with the knife. It is the man, who, for all his tommy-guns and rhetoric, is the innocent, inexplicably, compulsively and perpetually betrayed. Men and women have all but disappeared from our popular culture, leaving only this disturbing series of effigies with a motive power which we are told is sex, but which is actually a dream-like longing, an unfulfillment more wistful than that of the Sleeping Beauty awaiting the life-giving touch of the fated Prince. For the American dream of love insists that the Boy get the Girl; the tough guy has a disconcerting tendency to lapse abruptly into baby-talk and go off with Her—having first ascertained that she is not blood-guilty; and we are always told that this is what he *really* wants, to stop all this chasing around and settle down, to have children and a full life with a woman who, unhappily even when she appears, fails to exist. The merciless ingenuity of Mr. James M. Cain hit upon an effective solution to this problem in a recent novel by having his protagonist fall in love with a twelve year old, a female against whom no crime could be charged, who was not yet guilty of the shedding of blood and who thereafter kept herself pure for the hero until he returned from his exhausting improbable trials. This preposterous and tasteless notion did not seem, in Mr. Cain's world, to be preposterous or tasteless at all, but functioned, on the contrary, as an eminently fortunate and farsighted inspiration.

Mr. Cain, indeed, has achieved an enormous public and, I should hope, a not inconsiderable fortune on the basis of his remarkable preoccupation with the virile male. One may suggest that it was the dynamism of his material which trapped him into introducing, briefly, and with the air of a man wearing antiseptic gloves, an unattractive invert in an early novel, *Serenade,* who was promptly stabbed to death by the hero's mistress, a lusty and unlikely señorita. This novel contains a curious admission on the part of the hero to the effect that there is always somewhere a homosexual who can wear down the resistance of the normal man by knowing which buttons to press. This is presented as a serious and melancholy warning and it is when the invert of *Serenade* begins pressing too many buttons at once that he arrives at his sordid and bloody end. Thus is that immaculate manliness within us protected; thus summarily do we deal with any obstacle to the union of the Boy and the Girl. Can we doubt the wisdom of drawing the curtains when they finally come together? For the instant that the Boy and Girl become the Bride and Groom we are forced to leave them; not really supposing that the drama is over or that we have witnessed the fulfillment of two human beings, though we would like to believe this, but constrained by the knowledge that it is not for our eyes to witness the pain and the tempest that will follow. (For we *know* what follows; we know that life is not really like this at all.) What are we to say, who have already been betrayed, when this boy, this girl, discovers that the knife which preserved them for each other has unfitted them for experience? For the boy cannot know a woman since he has never become a man.

LABELS MUST BE SHATTERED

Hence, violence: that brutality which rages unchecked in our literature is part of the harvest of this unfulfillment, strident and dreadful testimony to our renowned and cherished innocence. Consider, in those extravagant denoucements which characterize those novels—to be more and more remarked on the bookselves—which are concerned with homosexuality, how high a value we place on this dangerous attribute. In *The City and the Pillar* [by Gore Vidal] the avowed homosexual who is the protagonist murders his first and only perfect love when at length they meet again for he cannot bear to kill instead that desolate and impossible dream of love which he has carried in his heart so long. In *The Folded Leaf* [by William Maxwell] the frail, introverted Lymie attempts suicide in an effort to escape the danger implicit in his love for Spud; a bloody act which, we are told, has purchased his maturity. In *The Fall of Valor* [by Charles Jackson] the god-like Marine defends his masculinity with a poker, leaving for dead the frightened professor who wanted him. These violent resolutions, all of them unlikely in the extreme, are compelled by a panic which is close to madness. These novels are not concerned with homosexuality but with the ever-present danger of sexual activity between men.

It is this unadmitted tension, longing and terror and wrath which creates their curiously mindless and pallid, yet smouldering atmosphere. It is a mistake, I think, that this subject matter sets them apart in any fruitful or significant way from anything written by James M. Cain or Laura Z. Hobson or Mary Jane Ward. They are alike in that they are wholly unable to recreate or interpret any of the reality or complexity of human experience; and that area which it is their self-avowed purpose to illuminate is precisely the area on which is thrown the most distorting light. As one may close *Gentleman's Agreement* [by Laura Keane Z. Hobson], which is about Gentiles and Jews, having gained no insight into the mind of either; as *The Snake Pit* [by Mary Jane Ward] reveals nothing of madness and James M. Cain tells us nothing of men and women, so one may read any current novel concerned with homosexual love and encounter merely a procession of platitudes the ancestry of which again may be traced to The Rover Boys [serialized novels by Arthur Winfield] and their golden ideal of chastity. It is quite impossible to write a worthwhile novel about a Jew or a Gentile or a Homosexual, for people refuse, unhappily, to function in so neat and one-dimensional a fashion. If the novelist considers that they are no more complex than their labels he must, of necessity, produce a catalogue, in which we will find, neatly listed, all those attributes with which the label is associated; and this can only operate to reinforce the brutal and dangerous anonymity of our culture.

A novel insistently demands the presence and passion of human beings, who cannot ever be labeled. Once the novelist has created a human being he has shattered the label and, in transcending the subject matter, is able, for the first time, to tell us something about it and to reveal how profoundly all things involving human beings interlock. Without this passion we may all smother to death, locked in those airless, labeled cells, which isolate us from each other and separate us from ourselves; and without this passion when we have discovered the connection between that Boy-Scout who smiles from the subway poster and that underworld to be found all over America, vengeful time will be upon us.

We Must Break Out of Our Individual Ghettos and Mobilize

LEO EBREO

In the concentration camps of Nazi Germany, homosexuals were imprisoned and murdered alongside Jews, prisoners of war, Gypsies, and alleged German traitors. As Nazi officer Heinrich Himmler remarked in 1937, "[The murder of homosexuals] was not punishment, more the simple elimination of this particular abnormality. It is vital we rid ourselves of them; like weeds we must pull them up, throw them on the fire and burn them. This is not out of a spirit of vengeance, but of necessity; these creatures must be exterminated." Similar dehumanizing thoughts and actions are what inspired the Jewish rights movement following World War II, a movement that Leo Ebreo saw as a model for the burgeoning gay rights movement of the 1960s.

By discussing his experience in the early Jewish rights movement and exploring the arguments raised against it, Ebreo offers the gay rights movement a way around such hurdles to more quickly galvanize the gay community and work toward securing their equal rights.

When I was younger—about sixteen—I was an active Zionist. I believed that the best thing for American Jews, in fact *all* Jews, to do would be to go to Israel and live in a kibbutz (collective). I belonged to a Zionist "movement" and tried to get the Jews I knew to join. I expected of course that few would want to emigrate, but I thought that most would be interested in helping Israel and the Zionist movement.

This was not the case. I was met, very often, by an extraordinary hostility. It was not until years later, reading works on Jewish self-hatred, Negro self-hatred, that I could realize that I had frightened some already-frightened people.

For this fright I have still no cure. The rational arguments which I gave my Jewish friends then, I would give them now.

These arguments (both the ones they gave me and my replies) came back to me recently when I began working in the homophile movement and speaking to homosexual friends about it. When I attempted to draw some parallel between the Jew's struggle for his rights and the homosexual's struggle for his, I was often stopped short with the explanation that there could be no parallel because one was a "religious problem" and the other a "sexual problem." I tried, without success, to show how much the Negro's struggle paralleled that of the Jew, even though the Negro "problem" was a "race problem" and not a "religious problem."

As I have said, I have no rational arguments against the surrender to fear, and the rejection of self that lies behind it. This essay is not written for those who have surrendered to fear, but for the others, the fighters.

I think we need to constantly reaffirm our perspective in the fight for homophile rights, to realize that we are part of a broad, general movement towards a better, freer, happier world.

This struggle of ours [in the 1960s] for complete acceptance will probably continue throughout our lifetime, as will the struggle of the Negro and the Jew. Oceans of hatred, unreason, rejection, craven fear will continue to come from the "other" world (of the white, the gentile, the heterosexual), will continue to infect many individuals within these oppressed minorities. . . .

A PARALLEL STRUGGLE—JEWISH LIBERATION

And in this light, I think my parallel Zionist experience will show us both the currents of the Opposition from within our own ranks, and the answers which we must make. The objections my Jewish friends raised were as follows:

(1) "I'm not that Jewish! Being Jewish isn't that important to me." (2) "I don't want to go to Israel." (3) "*You* are making the situation bad for *us*. There isn't any great problem. Discretion is the password. You are being offensive. You are putting us in a GHETTO, or would if we allowed you."...

CONFRONTING REALITY

And so, I think, it will be with those homosexual friends of mine who are now fearful, even resentful, of the homophile organizations. Their reactions now parallel, almost word for word, those of the Jews:

1. "I'm not that homosexual!" Here too, the image the outside world pictures is used by those raising this objection. One doesn't have to fit the stereotype to be *that* homosexual. (Yet to a certain extent we must work with the outside world's definition of the homosexual.) The German Jews were the most assimilated, often not knowing Yiddish, often not religious, often converted to Christianity. Still they were exterminated. Similarly, too often the one who suffers from persecution of homosexuals is the respectable married man, like [President Lyndon B. Johnson's aide Walter] Jenkins, who makes a single slip. [Jenkins was arrested in a "homosexual incident" at the District of Columbia YMCA.] No one trying to defend Jenkins (and there were few who did, to our eternal shame) noted that he wasn't *that* homosexual.

2. "I don't want to be a member of a homophile organization." My full sympathies. Neither do I. But I do belong, just as I belong to the United Jewish Appeal (UJA), to the National Association for the Advancement of Colored People (NAACP). Being in the Zionist movement, like being in the homophile movement, was to some extent a burden to me. It is a trial to pay dues, to attend meetings, to hear lectures, and— most of all—to have to deal with so many people and with their many, many faults. (St. Theresa, the Jewess of Avila, said that people were a great trial to her. That was the 16th cen-

tury, and people are still a great trial.) But don't you want the homophile movement to exist? Don't you want to see some organization represent homosexuals, stand up for their rights?

Fighting though I was for the state of Israel, I was still—and am still—a confirmed internationalist. But to arrive at that place in history, these intermediate steps are necessary. It is not

The Membership Pledge of the Mattachine Society—April 1951

While it is my conviction that homosexuality in our society is not a virtue but rather a handicap, I believe that I can live a well-oriented and socially productive life. I further believe the social ostracism and legal persecution of homosexuals can be minimized or eliminated through the Mattachine Society which is organized to influence the conduct of homosexuals themselves, and to formulate and develop a social, positive, body of ethic for the homosexual. I shall live and work to the end that, through these principles, I myself shall become a better person, and through my work and my self-improvement the Mattachine Society shall be that much more enabled to aid an enlightened society to accept my people as useful and valuable citizens.

The Missions and Purposes of the Mattachine Society have been explained to me in detail, and I understand and accept them as my own. In order to further these missions and purposes, I take the following pledge without reservation or qualifications:

I PLEDGE MYSELF—

(1) always to keep the interests of the Mattachine Society uppermost in my mind and to conduct myself in a way that will reflect credit upon myself and the organization;

a certain good—an absolute good—that there be a state of Israel, with borders, army, taxes, ministries. But until there are no French, German, Russian, American nationalities, I think it unwise to eliminate the Jewish nationality, which all these nations have at times acknowledged (before its official creation) by discriminating against it.

(2) in every possible way, to respect the rights of all racial, religious, and national minorities, since I realize that I also am a member of a persecuted minority;

(3) to try to observe the generally accepted social rules of dignity and propriety at all times . . . in my conduct, attire, and speech;

(4) to strive in every possible way to interest other responsible people in the Mattachine Society and to recruit members for the organization without regard to their race, color, or creed;

(5) to participate actively and seriously in the work, responsibilities, and functions of the Society;

(6) unconditionally, to guard the anonymity of all members of the Mattachine Society, of sponsoring organization and affiliates; and, in the event I ever leave the organization for any reason whatsoever, I pledge myself to guard the anonymity of the membership, sponsoring organizations and affiliates, throughout my entire life.

I have read this pledge carefully and thoughtfully, and I understand it completely. In the presence of these members of the Mattachine Society, I do, here, and now, of my own free will and volition, and after careful thought and reason, solemnly swear to uphold this pledge which admits me to membership in the Organization.

Mark Blasius and Shane Phelan, *We Are Everywhere: A Historical Sourcebook of Gay and Lesbian Politics.* New York: Routledge, 1997, p. 284.

The question you must ask yourself is not whether you "like" to join or at least support a homophile organization (or a civil rights organization), but whether it is *needed*. And the homophile movement is needed, as Israel is needed, *at this point in history.*

THE FEAR OF GHETTOIZATION

3. "Your homophile organizations make our situation worse. . . . Discretion is the password. You are being offensive. You are putting homosexuals in a ghetto." Here again we are dealing often with homosexual fear and self-hatred and self-rejection.

This very word—GHETTO—has been used to me by homosexuals outside the movement. The homosexual who says this has accepted the negative picture of the homosexual drawn by the outside world. And, just as the American Jew may imagine a nation of candy store keepers with Yiddish accents and skullcaps, so the "assimilated" homosexual, from his troglodyte perspective, may imagine an assembly of campy ballet dancers and hairdressers.

There is already something of a ghetto pattern for homosexuals, because of the pressures put on them to confine themselves to certain vocations where they are "expected" and to isolate themselves.

But the aim of the homophile organizations, like that of the NAACP, the UJA, is not for further ghettoization but for *integration*, for *equality.*

A GHETTO OF ONE

However, there is a radical difference between the situation of the homosexual and that of the Negro and Jew in relation to their organizations. The Negro can rarely "pass." The Jew might be able to, but he is under many pressures, especially family upbringing and sometimes family presence, not to. The homosexual, on the other hand, can usually "pass" easily and does not have the family pressure as an inducement to declare himself. If anything, there is another pressure, to "pass" for the sake of family appearances.

Thus the individual homosexual may claim that membership in a homophile organization, rather than enabling him to normalize his situation, might endanger the assimilation, the equality he can achieve with just a bit of "discretion" and silence. This argument has a certain cogency. Its limitation is that it is a solution for the *individual* homosexual.

It is the "solution" (or, to be charitable, the "path") taken by the average homosexual, especially the one outside a major city, or who is not in touch with the gay community. And this is not a solution, a path, which is to be avoided. For certain people, in positions in the government, in schools, there may be no choice but secrecy at this time.

But the price can be a terrible one. It is, as I have said, an individual solution. Often, too often, it results in an isolation for the individual, sometimes a world of pathetic furtive sexuality or public lavatory sex—shameful, inadequate, ridiculous, dangerous. Even when the hidden homosexual has a mate, the union still has a peculiar isolate character, being secret, disguised. Thus the homosexual who "passes" is often in a ghetto composed of one person, sometimes of two. An individual solution perhaps, but hardly a permanent one, or a good one.

BREAKING OUT OF THE GHETTO

Those of us who are active in the homophile movement feel ourselves working for those outside and fearful of joining. We are working for a day when our organizations will be strong enough, active enough, to protect the rights of those in public employment (such as teachers), in the armed services, in government. The homosexual who is accepted as a homosexual will be a fuller, better person than the furtive imitation-heterosexual who has found his individual "solution."

The aim of the homophile organizations is not to draw a small circle and place the homosexual within it. The very term "homosexual" (only 68 years old if we are to believe the Oxford English Dictionary) may not be used with such frequency in the Larger Society which we are working to create. We *are* drawing a circle—but a LARGE circle, to draw the large society of which we are a part, in. We are asking to be accepted. This acceptance which the homosexual minority needs, wants, can only be gotten when it is *asked* for—if need be, DEMON-STRATED for through groups like East Coast Homophile Organizations (ECHO) and their picket lines.

The drive to eliminate discrimination against homosexuals (sex fascism) is a direct parallel to the drive to eliminate discrimination against Negroes (race fascism). These minority movements are not attempts to overthrow the white race, or to destroy the institution of the family, but to allow a fuller growth of human potential, breaking down the barriers against a strange race or sexuality. When the Negro, the Jew, the homosexual, is known and a neighbor, he will cease to be a bogey.

We are working towards that world in which there will be respect for, enjoyment of, the differences in nationality, race, sexuality, when the homosexual impulse is seen as part of the continuum of love which leads some persons to be husbands and wives, others to be parents, others to be lovers of their fellow men and women, and still others to be celibate and devote themselves to humanity or deity.

In that world there will also be greater variety. Our stratified ideas of masculinity and femininity will long have been altered. (Have you noticed that men's greeting cards have either a gun and mallard ducks, or a fishing rod and trout?)

It is this world, where the barriers of nation, sex, race have been broken, this larger, non-ghettoized world, that minority groups are organizing to work toward. And it is this picture of the larger world of the future that we must hold up when we are accused, by the very existence of homophile organizations at this point in history, of wanting to ghettoize homosexuals.

"Knock, and it shall be opened unto you."

Sexism Within the Growing Movement

SHIRLEY WILLER

In the 1950s activists founded two major gay rights organizations—
the Mattachine Society and the more radical ONE, which had a less
apologetic tone in arguing that homosexuality was positive and life-
affirming. However, a third organization—the Daughters of Bilitis
(DOB)—was the first lesbian organization in the United States. The
group's name came from a book of poetry written by a man, which
described love among Sappho's school (Sappho was a Greek poet
who often wrote of her love of other women), an irony surely not
lost on DOB members who felt that gay men didn't recognize lesbians' concerns but expected their full support in a movement that
at the time lacked female leadership.

The following selection, from former DOB president Shirley
Willer, explores what it meant to be a lesbian in the 1960s, touch-
ing in particular on the issue of sexism within the movement. Willer
ends on a note of promise, however, by proposing four goals to
strengthen not only lesbian activism but the gay rights movement as
a whole.

To an extent it is difficult for me to discuss what the homophile movement should be doing. I have some very
clear ideas about what the Lesbian should be doing but the
problems of the male homosexual and the female homosexual differ considerably.

Most perceptive authorities have stated that the basic problems in relations between the sexes arise from the completely
artificial dichotomies of role and appearance ascribed to each
sex by society. From the median beds wherein we lie, few

Shirley Willer, "What Concrete Steps Can Be Taken to Further the Homophile Movement?" *The Ladder*, vol. 11, 1996, pp. 17–20. Copyright © 1996 by *The Ladder*. Reproduced by permission.

ORIGINS OF THE GAY RIGHTS MOVEMENT • 57

persons, homosexual or heterosexual, arise whole and healthy individuals.

The social conformist is wracked by anxieties in his ambivalent clinging to the social artifacts which require his denunciation of his nature. The social non-conformist is driven to propound his personal revelation as being above reproach and beyond question. In such a society Lesbian interest is more closely linked with the women's civil rights movement than the homosexual civil liberties movement.

BEING HOMOSEXUAL AND FEMALE

The particular problems of the male homosexual include police harassment, unequal law enforcement, legal proscription of sexual practices and for a relatively few the problem of disproportionate penalties for acts of questionable taste such as evolve from solicitations, wash-room sex acts and transsexual attire.

In contrast, few women are subject to police harassment and the instances of arrest of Lesbians for solicitation, wash-room sex or transsexual attire are so infrequent as to constitute little threat to the Lesbian community beyond the circle of the immediately involved. The rare occurrences serve to remind the Lesbian that such things are possible, but also that they rarely happen.

The problems of importance to the Lesbian are job security, career advancement and family relationships.

The important difference between the male and female homosexual is that the Lesbian is discriminated against not only because she is a Lesbian, but because she is a woman. Although the Lesbian occupies a "privileged" place among homosexuals, she occupies an under-privileged place in the world.

A MOVEMENT DIVIDED BY GENDER

It is difficult for a woman to be accepted as a leader in any community or civic organization and the woman who does succeed in breaking down the barriers in recognition is usually greeted with a mixture of astonishment and sympathetic amusement. There are few women who desire to emulate Carrie Nation [a member of the Women's Christian Temperance Union], chained to a fire hydrant and swinging a battle-axe— but the few women who achieve community, professional or civic leadership are compared to that image, sometimes rightfully so, since despite legal recognition of feminine equality, the road to public recognition for each woman leads across the battlefield.

Lesbians have agreed (with reservations) to join in common cause with the male homosexual—her role in society has been one of mediator between the male homosexual and society. The recent (1966) Daughters of Bilitis (DOB) Convention was such a gesture. The reason we were able to get the public officials there was because we are women, because we offered no threat. However, they did not bargain for what they got. They did not expect to be challenged on the issues of male homosexuality. In these ways we show our willingness to assist the male homosexual in seeking to alleviate the problems our society has inflicted on him.

There has been little evidence however, that the male homosexual has any intention of making common cause with us. We suspect that should the male homosexual achieve his particular objectives in regard to his homosexuality he might possibly become a more adamant foe of women's rights than the heterosexual male has ever been. (I would guess that a preponderance of male homosexuals would believe their ultimate goal achieved if the laws relating to sodomy were removed and a male homosexual were appointed chief of police.)

WE MUST ADDRESS DIVERSE CONCERNS

This background may help you understand why, although the Lesbian joins the male homosexual in areas of immediate and common concern, she is at the same time preparing for a longer struggle, waged on a broader base with the widest possible participation of the rank and file Lesbian. It shows why, to the Lesbian leader, diffusion and consensus are as important as leadership and direction. Demonstrations which define the homosexual as a unique minority defeat the very cause for which the homosexual strives—*TO BE CONSIDERED AN INTEGRAL PART OF SOCIETY.* The homosexual must show that he is, in fact, *NOT* a unique "social problem." That concept is too widely held to require endorsement from homophile organizations. Demonstrations that emphasize the uniqueness of the homosexual may provide an outlet for some homosexuals' hostilities, but having acted out his revolt, he loses a part of the drive that might have been available for more constructive approaches to problem solving.

The basic objectives of the homophile organizations must continue to be open to new avenues of in-depth communication. Its energies must not be channelized—its attempts must be repetitive—its approaches must be as diverse as imagination will allow. To put this more specifically, *THE MORE WAYS WE CAN GET MORE PEOPLE INVOLVED IN THE GREATEST VARIETY OF APPROACHES TO THE WIDEST POSSIBLE CONFIGURATION OF THE PROBLEMS RELATED TO HOMOSEXUALITY, THE MORE LIKELY WE ARE TO ACHIEVE SOME MEASURE OF SUCCESS.*

I can name a few dozen of the concrete steps your organizations should be taking. I do not doubt that you have tried them. Then, I say continue these and add more and more and more.

The argument that concentration is more productive than diversity is false when applied to homophile organizations. You cannot "retool" the talents of your membership to meet a current market. The only thing you may do is warehouse talent which could be of use to the common cause. Because this is a fact, one also hears the notion that instead of retooling the members, we should retool the organizations and perhaps, eventually, each person will find the organization of his level and interest.

TOWARD A UNITED FRONT

Accordingly, proceeding from our statement of [intent] we wish to offer a few constructive steps—steps we do not like to call concrete, but in full knowledge of the shifts of time and structure, we believe to be firm and tread-worthy.

1. To affirm as a goal of such a conference: to be as concerned about women's civil rights as male homosexuals' civil liberties.

2. To suggest that homosexual men attempt to appreciate the value of women as *PEOPLE* in the movement, respect abilities as individuals, not seek them out as simple "show-pieces."

3. That those philosophical factors of homosexuality which engage both sexes be basic to our concepts of reform.

4. That the number of one sex not be a determinate factor in decisions of policy, but that a consideration of all arguments be heard and that *CONSENSUS* be the goal of the conference. Insofar as we do find trust and value in the male-oriented homophile organizations, we will find common ground upon which to work.

CHAPTER 2

COMING OUT AND COMING TOGETHER

AMERICAN
SOCIAL
MOVEMENTS

How the Stonewall Inn Uprising Politicized the Gay Community

JACK NICHOLS

Jack Nichols is the senior editor at GayToday.com and author of *The Gay Agenda: Talking Back to Fundamentalists.* In the following selection—part of Gay Today's history project—Nichols describes his experiences in New York's gay culture of the 1960s. In particular he contrasts the days before and after the infamous Stonewall Inn riot in 1969, noting how gay conservatives reacted to the new breed of militant activists born of the riots.

The Stonewall Inn, a dive bar and disco in New York City, was frequented by drag queens and street people. On June 28, 1969, police raided the inn allegedly for operating without a liquor license. As they began to check identifications and make arrests, the inn's patrons began to file out onto the street. They then did something unexpected both by the police as well as themselves—they fought back. They hurled change and other objects at the police and Molotov cocktails at the bar. In the words of activist Sylvia (Ray) Rivera, who participated in the melee, "I thought, 'My god, the revolution is here. The revolution is finally here.'"

Stonewall brought a new urgency to the gay rights movement that was not, however, shared by all. As Nichols observes, "Almost immediately, it became clear there were those who would integrate gays into the mainstream culture and those who believed that culture to be unredeemable." While the movement has made great strides in the past few decades, this schism between gay conservatives and more militant activists continues to rage on.

The Stonewall Inn [on Christopher Street in Greenwich Village, New York City], between 1967–1969, was often a fun place.

I recall a free-wheeling, colorful and democratic scene attracting a great variety of types, especially long-haired youths trying—as youths often do—to get away from their otherwise "proper" home environments and meeting gladdened refugees in flight from pre-69 Manhattan's generally unappealing gay bar circuit.

Only a few years before, I'd frequented the *Ce Soir,* one of Gotham's two gay "dance" bars where, in a back room, a light bulb hung ominously from a single cord, ignited whenever an unknown customer entered the front door.

The lighting of the bulb signaled that dancing couples must separate. In June, 1969 The Stonewall Inn was light years away from this furtive past, attracting the arrival of what media soon began calling "the new homosexual," emboldened by the 60's counterculture, by new standards challenging gender roles. Pot—the good weed—was, in those days, the drug of choice.

It was under the influence of this organic substance, in fact, that many contemplated the social revolution going on around them. It inspired assaults on inhibitions and encouraged the bold to denounce a frigid past, to look toward the creation of a new world consciousness.

Hippies, a gentle, loving, environmentally conscious, Zen-reading, LSD-gobbling, sexually communal, non-judgmental, non-violent critical mass, had upset the apple cart of social decorum. There was hope in their eyes, hope for a better future. . . .

CONSERVATIVES HINDERED UNIFICATION

My own late-Sixties early-Seventies experience confirmed this boy's perspective. I began hoping—in contrast to ghetto separatists—for a final melting of gay/straight divisions and the creation of a sexually integrated society in which everybody would be free to love and make love without self-identifying through specialized sexual labels. I hoped that the developing demand for the equalization of the sexes would help bring such a world into being.

The counterculture revolution was seen by gay conservatives and by right wing politicos as a threat to the social order. The gay conservatives sought a world in which previously acceptable heterosexual standards were to be implemented in gay circles. They established gay Christian churches, sought to have their own children not through adoptions but through artificial inseminations, suggested imitation establishment marriages, and asked, along with heterosexual males, the right to fight and kill for a belligerent Vietnam-punishing Uncle Sam.

The conservatives we have with us always.

But the straight counterculture, and "the new homosexuals" were going, during the Vietnam war, in another direction, declaring themselves "gay" at the draft boards to muddle conscriptions and to denounce the war. . . .

"THE NEW HOMOSEXUALS" AND GAY PRIDE

Lige Clarke was, like me, a gay counterculture type. His observations on matrimoniacs and the crumbling institution of marriage, his concerns for suffering, starving children in an overpopulated world; his disdain for the prudish Richard Nixon and for the silly self-righteousness of established powers like the churches; his experience of the wasteful Pentagon (where he'd previously edited, with 11 security clearances, top secret messages in the office of the Army Joint Chief of Staff), made his views quite different, as were mine, from that of the gay assimilationists.

Our militant gay activism had preceded the Stonewall uprising by nearly a decade. In 1965 we'd launched picketing in Washington's direct action group, the Mattachine Society. But it was a foiled police raid on the Stonewall Inn in late June, 1969 [allegedly for liquor being served without a license], that first caught the media's attention. The Stonewall uprising offered just the right mix of dramatics: youths fighting back for the first time against police corruption, the stuff of a legend.

Almost immediately, it became clear there were those who would integrate gays into the mainstream culture and those who believed that culture to be unredeemable. As gay columnists writing for the then-zany SCREW, an otherwise straight tabloid, and for the gay newspaper, *The Advocate,* Lige Clarke and I wrote the first journalist's published accounts of the Stonewall rebellion and, because of our counterculture underpinnings, we not only celebrated it, but called on the youths of our time to press the Stonewall uprising beyond its narrow boundaries. On July 8, 1969, sounding the counterculture's view, we issued this "call to arms":

> *The homosexual revolution is only part of a larger revolution sweeping through all segments of society. We hope that "Gay Power" will not become a call for separation, but for sexual integration, and that the young activists will read, study, and make themselves acquainted with all of the facts which will help them to carry the sexual revolt triumphantly into the councils of the U.S. government, into the anti-homosexual churches, into the offices of anti-homosexual psychiatrists, into the city government, and into the state legislatures which make our manner of lovemaking a crime. It is time to push the homosexual revolution to its logical conclusion. We must crush tyranny wherever it exists and join forces with those who would assist in the utter destruction of the puritanical, repressive, anti-sexual Establishment.*

DEFENDING SEXUALITY OF ALL KINDS

We spoke, at the time, not so much of a homosexual revolution but of a revolt much larger in scope, one that addressed underlying problems like America's general difficulty facing as an extremely positive phenomenon, sexuality of all kinds. John Loughery, in his award-winning and exquisitely written history of the gay 20th century *The Other Side of Silence,* explained part of what we aimed to accomplish:

> *"This was part of a 'vision of liberation,' as novelist Michael*

Rumaker wrote, encompassing more than gay rights: 'The larger vision was the death of flesh hatred and shame.'"

We hoped to see (fulfilled non-coercively) every person's natural sexual curiosity instead of its being a source of embarrassment and titillation. Pornography and possibly rape, we thought, could only thrive where sexual repression remained rampant.

"Make Love Not War," was much more than just a slogan

Drag Queens and Street People: Heroes of the Stonewall Uprising

The Stonewall Inn (next door to the present New York bar by that name) was a shabby dive that served watered-down drinks in glasses that were questionably sanitary. It wasn't really a drag queen's bar. Only a certain number of drag queens were allowed in at a time and only if they were known by the owners.

Was it [the Stonewall Uprising] led by gay leaders who drank expensive wine, read best-selling books, could afford to attend expensive fundraisers, hob-knobbed with politicians, and invested wisely? No.

As if to throw the whole issue of Lesbian, Gay, Bi-sexual, and Transgender (LGBT) classism in our faces, it was led by drag queens and street people. The symbol of our liberation is not the cultured and coiffed but the least understood and the down on their luck, the people looked down upon by others as lazy, dirty, and "low class."

"The Legend of the Stonewall Inn: What Does It Mean?" www.gaytoday.com, June 17, 2002.

of the times. As a counterculture theme it said that sexual repression and moronic macho posing must be dismissed because the frustrations resulting from these were root causes of a widespread militaristic mania.

Violence, in other words, was defined as the great obscenity. Former Secretary of Defense Robert McNamara's belated confession—that he'd always known that the war he'd championed was unwinnable—seems now to have justified this definition of violence. Dr. Martin Luther King, Jr.—in the midst of the government's military madness—had insisted that unconditional love would "have the final word in reality."

But America's conservative establishment would not be easily swayed, in spite of the many signs that pointed to needed change. Traditional institutions armed with vast financial resources, went on the offense, re-grouping against this splendid challenge to their oppressive programs. They would later work to discredit and muddle the counterculture's saving visions expressed through its gurus such as Theodore Rozak, Paul Goodman and Alan Watts. . . .

GAY LIBERATION, NOT ASSIMILATION

Following on the heels of avant garde feminism and the successes of the black civil rights movement, gay liberation began, after Stonewall, to gain some measure of wary recognition from a media that had deliberately ignored the earlier more peaceful picketing demonstrations at the White House, Independence Hall, the Pentagon, the Civil Service Commission and the State Department.

Michael Bakunin's anarchist slogan, "None of us are free till all of us are free," reverberated in the meetings of New York's Gay Liberation Front (GLF), established on the heels of the Stonewall rebellion. I was heartened by this, but soon became disheartened when I saw GLF fall prey to dogmatists who effectively split the energies of its idealistic membership.

The Gay Activist Alliance (GAA), (contrary to impressions given in revisionist, error-riddled histories like Martin Duberman's *Stonewall*) inherited those Stonewall energies, and GLF largely disappeared from the New York scene.

GAA, on the other hand, focused on the gay issue alone, and in a series of daring "zaps" [nonviolent, face-to-face confrontations with government and civil leaders considered homophobic] served notice through direct action that a new era was at hand. There were those of us interested in other causes and who saw how gay issues connected with them but to the Stonewall era's generation of activists, focus on gay issues, needed after long and impossible silences, seemed essential.

CAN WE MOVE BEYOND THE STATUS QUO?

I made my peace with my more conservative friends by saying that the gay counterculture, on the one hand, and gay assimilationists on the other made, perhaps, two sides of a coin that, once spent, would pave the way for all same-sex lovers toward greener pastures.

But I've remained, through the years and even in the face of the gay and lesbian movement's major successes, sorry that the clear voice of the counterculture—questioning established institutions—has been mostly drowned out by a more vocal gay establishment seeking acceptance among the power players in the status quo. One of the singular values of gay liberation, therefore, gets lost, specifically its being a catalyst and encouraging, as it should for anybody who thinks about what the gay struggle reveals, skepticism about the shaky-idea foundation stones supporting the status quo. . . .

Today I marvel when I see what's been accomplished in a mere 30 years since the Stonewall uprising. Since that first gay march at The White House in 1965, when only ten people—three women and seven men (including myself)—took part, I've watched our capital city's gay and lesbian demonstrations grow size-wise over the decades—expanding into what we only dreamed about early on. I've seen a U.S. President speak out repeatedly on behalf of same-sex love and affection, and I've seen a giant community of gay men and lesbians rally to care for the sick and the wounded in this World War Three against AIDS.

Even if it is, in certain ways, a sexually-segregated community still, I continue to hope for a much-integrated future where, as prophesied by Walt Whitman, men will blur distinctions by walking hand in hand in America's streets because, as he well knew, same-sex love is not a gay matter alone, no, *"the germ is in everybody."*

The Effeminist Manifesto

STEVEN DANSKY, JOHN KNOEBEL, AND KENNETH PITCHFORD

The "Effeminist Manifesto," which first appeared in *Double-F: A Magazine of Effeminism* in 1971, is one of the most enduring documents to emerge from the modern gay liberation movement. It fermented controversy in the gay movement by questioning the sexism of gay men, by proposing that all men oppress women, and by challenging subcultural adjustment of gay men to the prevailing patriarchal society. Foremost, the "Effeminist Manifesto" proposed that men could be profeminist—and the term *Effeminist* was conceived to designate those men who supported the women's movement.

This polemic debate extended from gay liberation into the mainstream media. Jill Johnston in the *Village Voice* said that "Effeminists are the first western male revolutionaries. The first men to confess the inappropriateness of their manhood and to withdraw from the classic male demand of support from the female." Martin Duberman declared in the *New York Times Book Review*, that Effeminists "are formulating basic questions on gender." The "Effeminist Manifesto" questioned basic assumptions about gender, and so it remains relevant decades after it was written.

Steven Dansky, a founder of the modern gay movement, responded to the urgency of the HIV/AIDS pandemic as an activist, psychotherapist, and author of the books *Now Dare Everything: Tales of HIV-Related Psychotherapy* (Haworth Press, 1994) and *Nobody's Children: Orphans of the HIV Epidemic* (Haworth Press, 1997). John Knoebel spent sixteen years as a senior executive with the national gay and lesbian newsmagazine the *Advocate* and is now a nationally recognized expert on the gay and lesbian market as president of the gay marketing firm Triangle Marketing Services. Kenneth Pitchford, a contributor to *Oxford Poetry*, published a translation of Rainer Maria Rilke's, *Sonnets to Orpheus* (Purchase Press, 1981), and *Color Photos of the Atrocities* (Little, Brown & Company, 1973). Dansky, Knoebel, and Pitchford live in New York.

*W*e, *the undersigned Effeminists of DOUBLE-F* [a magazine of effeminism] *hereby invite all like minded men to join with us in making our Declaration of Independence from Gay Liberation & all other Male Ideologies by unalterably asserting our stand of revolutionary commitment to the following Thirteen Principles that form the quintessential substance of our politics:*

THE PRINCIPLES OF REVOLUTIONARY EFFEMINISM

On the oppression of women.

1. *SEXISM.* All women are oppressed by all men, including ourselves. This systematic oppression is called sexism.

2. *MALE SUPREMACY.* Sexism itself is the product of male supremacy, which produces all the other forms of oppression that patriarchal societies exhibit: racism, classism, ageism, economic exploitation, ecological imbalance.

3. *GYNARCHISM.* Only that revolution that strikes at the root of all oppression can end any and all of its forms. That is why we are gynarchists; that is, we are among those who believe that women will seize power from the patriarchy and, thereby, totally change life on this planet as we know it.

4. *WOMEN'S LEADERSHIP.* Exactly how women will go about seizing power is no business of ours, being men. But as effeminate men oppressed by masculinist standards, we ourselves have a stake in the destruction of the patriarchy, and thus we *must* struggle with the dilemma of being partisans—as effeminists—of a revolution opposed to us—as men. To conceal our partisanship and remain inactive for fear of offending would be despicable; to act independently of women's leadership or to tamper with questions which women will decide would be no less despicable. Therefore, we have a duty to take sides, to struggle to change ourselves—but also, necessarily, to act.

On the oppression of effeminate men.

5. *MASCULINISM.* Faggots and all effeminate men are oppressed by the patriarchy's systematic enforcement of masculinist standards, whether these standards are expressed as physical, mental, emotional, or sexual stereotypes of what is desirable in a man.

6. *EFFEMINISM.* Our purpose is to urge all such men as ourselves (whether celibate, homosexual, or heterosexual) to become traitors to the class of men by uniting in a movement of Revolutionary Effeminism so that collectively we can struggle to change ourselves from non-masculinists into anti-masculinists and begin attacking those aspects of the patriarchal system that most directly oppress us.

7. *PREVIOUS MALE IDEOLOGIES.* Three previous attempts by men to create a politics for fighting oppression have failed because of their incomplete analysis: the Male Left, Male Liberation, and Gay Liberation. These and other formulations, such as sexual libertarianism and the counterculture, are all tactics for preserving power in men's hands by pretending to struggle for change. We specifically reject a carry-over from one or more of these earlier ideologies—the damaging combination of ultra-egalitarianism, anti-leadership, anti-technology, and downward mobility. All are based on a politics of guilt and a hypocritical attitude toward power which prevents us from developing skills urgently needed in our struggle and which confuses the competence needed for revolutionary work with the careerism of those who seek personal accommodation within the patriarchal system.

8. *COLLABORATORS AND CAMP-FOLLOWERS.* Even we effeminate men are given an option by the patriarchy: to become collaborators in the task of keeping women in their place. Faggots, especially, are offered a subculture by the patriarchy which is designed to keep us oppressed and also increase the oppression of women. This subculture includes a combination of anti-woman mimicry and self-mockery known as camp which, with its trivializing effect, would deny us any chance of awakening to our own suffering, the expres-

sion of which is called madness by the patriarchy, but which can be recognized as revolutionary sanity by the oppressed.

9. *SADO-MASCULINITY: ROLE PLAYING AND OB-JECTIFICATION.* The Male Principle, as exhibited in the last ten thousand years, is chiefly characterized by an appetite for objectification, role-playing, and sadism. First, the masculine preference for thinking as opposed to feeling encourages men to regard other people as things, and to use them accordingly.

The Goals of the Gay Liberation Front in Europe

The long-term goal of Gay Liberation, which inevitably brings us into conflict with the institutionalised sexism of this society, is to rid society of the gender-role system which is at the root of our oppression. This can only be achieved by eliminating the social pressures on men and women to conform to narrowly defined gender roles. It is particularly important that children and young people be encouraged to develop their own talents and interests and to express their own individuality rather than act out stereotyped parts alien to their nature.

As we cannot carry out this revolutionary change alone, and as the abolition of gender roles is also a necessary condition of women's liberation, we will work to form a strategic alliance with the women's liberation movement, aiming to develop our ideas and our practice in close inter-relation. In order to build this alliance, the brothers in gay liberation will have to be prepared to sacrifice that degree of male chauvinism and male privilege that they still all possess.

To achieve our long term goal will take many years, perhaps decades. But attitudes to the appropriate place of men and women in our society are changing rapidly, par-

Second, inflicting pain upon people and animals has come to be deemed a mark of manhood, thereby explaining the well-known proclivity for rape and torture. Finally, a lust for power-dominance is rewarded in the playing out of that ultimate role. The Man, whose rapacity is amply displayed in witch-hunts, lynchings, pogroms, and episodes of genocide, not to mention the day-to-day (often life-long) subservience that he exacts from those closest to him.

ticularly the belief in the subordinate place for women. Modern conditions are placing increasing strain on the small nuclear family containing one adult male and one adult female with narrowly defined roles and bound together for life.

The starting point of our liberation must be to rid ourselves of the oppression which lies in the head of every one of us. This means freeing our heads from self oppression and male chauvinism, and no longer organising our lives according to the patterns with which we are indoctrinated by straight society. It means that we must *root out* the idea that homosexuality is bad, sick or immoral, and develop a gay *pride*. In order to survive, most of us have either knuckled under to pretend that no oppression exists, and the result of this has been further to distort our heads. Within gay liberation, a number of consciousness-raising groups have already developed, in which we try to understand our oppression and learn new ways of thinking and behaving. The aim is to step outside the experience permitted by straight society, and to learn to love and trust one another. This is the precondition for acting and struggling together.

First printed by Russell Press (Nottingham, England) and then revised in 1979 and reprinted by Gay Liberation Information Service (London). Found online at *People with a History*. Ed. Paul Halsall. www.fordham.edu/halsall/pwh/glf-london.html.

Masculine bias, thus, appears in our behavior whenever we act out the following categories, regardless of which element in each pair we are most drawn to at any given moment: subject/object; dominant/submissive; master/slave; butch/femme. All of these false dichotomies are inherently sexist, since they express the desire to be masculine or to possess the masculine in someone else. The racism of white faggots often reveals the same set of polarities, regardless of whether they choose to act out the dominant or submissive role with black or third-world men. In all cases, only by rejecting the very terms of these categories can we become effeminists. This means explicitly rejecting, as well, the objectification of people based on such things as age; body build; color, size, or shape of facial features, eyes, hair, genitals, ethnicity or race; physical or mental handicap; life-style; sex. We must therefore strive to detect and expose every embodiment of The Male Principle, no matter how and where it may be enshrined and glorified, including those arenas of faggot objectification (baths, bars, docks, parks) where power-dominance, as it operates in the selecting of roles and objects, is known as "cruising."

10. *MASOCH-EONISM.* Among those aspects of our oppression which The Man has foisted upon us, two male heterosexual perversions, in particular, are popularly thought of as being "acceptable" behavior for effeminate men: eonism (that is, male transvestitism) and masochism. Just as sadism and masculinism, by merging into one identity, tend to become indistinguishable one from the other, so masochism and eonism are born of an identical impulse toward mock subservience in men, as a way to project intense anti-woman feelings and also to pressure women into conformity by providing those degrading stereotypes most appealing to the sado-masculinist. Certainly, sado-masoch-eonism in all its forms is the very antithesis of effeminism. Both the masochist and the eonist are particularly an insult to women since they overtly parody female oppression and pose as object lessons in servility.

11. *LIFE-STYLE: APPEARANCE AND REALITY.* We must learn to discover and value The Female Principle in men

as something inherent, beyond roles or superficial decoration, and thus beyond definition by any one particular life-style (such as the recent androgyny fad, transsexuality, or other purely personal solutions). Therefore, we do not automatically support or condemn faggots or effeminists who live alone, who live together as couples, who live together in all-male collectives, who live with women, or who live in any other way—since all of these modes of living in and of themselves can be sexist but can also conceivably come to function as bases for anti-sexist struggle. Even as we learn to affirm in ourselves the cooperative impulse and to admire in each other what is tender and gentle, what is aesthetic, considerate, affectionate, lyrical, sweet, we should not confuse our own time with that post-revolutionary world when our effeminist natures will be free to express themselves openly without fear of punishment or danger of oppressing others. Above all, we must remember that it is not merely a change of appearance that we seek, but a change in reality.

12. *TACTICS.* We mean to support, defend, and promote effeminism in all men everywhere by any means except those inherently male supremacist or those in conflict with the goals of feminists intent on seizing power. We hope to find militant ways for fighting our oppression that will meet these requirements. Obviously, we do not seek the legalization of faggotry, quotas or civil-rights for faggots, or other measures designed to reform the patriarchy. Practically, we see three phases of activity: naming our enemies to start with, next confronting them, and ultimately divesting them of their power. This means both the Cock Rocker and the Drag Rocker among counter-cultist heroes, both the Radical Therapist and the Faggot-Torturer among effemiphobic psychiatrists, both the creators of beefcake pornography and of eonistic travesties. It also means all branches of the patriarchy that institutionalize the persecution of faggots (school, church, army, prison, asylum, old-age home).

But whatever the immediate target, we would be wise to prepare for all forms of sabotage and rebellion which women might ask of us, since it is not as pacifists that we can expect to serve in the emerging worldwide anti-gender revolution. We must also constantly ask ourselves and each other for a greater measure of risk and commitment than we may have dreamt was possible yesterday. Above all, our joining in this struggle must discover in us a new respect for women, a new ability to love each other as effeminists, both of which have previously been denied us by our own misogyny and effemiphobia, so that our bonding until now has been the traditional male solidarity that is always inimical to the best interests of women and pernicious to our own sense of effeminist selfhood, as well.

13. *DRUDGERY AND CHILDCARE: RE-DEFINING GENDER.* Our first and most important step, however, must be to take upon ourselves at least our own share of the day-to-day life-sustaining drudgery that is usually consigned to women alone. To be useful in this way can release women to do other work of their own choosing and can also begin to redefine gender for the next generation. Of paramount concern here, we ask to be included in the time consuming work of raising and caring for children, as a duty, a right, and a privilege.

Attested to this twenty-seventh day of Teves and first day of January, in the year of our faltering Judeo-Christian patriarchy, 5733 and 1973.

Harvey Milk's Political Empowerment of the Gay Community

GREGORY J. ROSMAITA

Author Gregory J. Rosmaita presents an overview of the life and politics of Harvey Milk, the first openly gay elected city official. In 1977, Milk won a seat on the San Francisco Board of Supervisors, and fought passionately to protect the civil rights of his constituents and preserve the city's economic vitality for future generations. What made him unique, however, was that Milk was never a professional politician; he remained free of obligations to any party or platform.

Rosmaita also notes the enormous sense of responsibility Milk felt toward the gay community: "Milk's goal in asserting gay pride through political empowerment was not to force mainstream America to accept homosexuality, but to respect the homosexual's right to be homosexual, without governmental interference or hindrance." Unfortunately, fellow supervisor Dan White did not agree with Milk and felt that Milk had blocked his reappointment because of White's anti-gay leaning. (White had resigned to take a higher-paying job but then changed his mind and wanted his job back.) On November 27, 1978, White went to the San Francisco City Hall where he not only shot and killed Milk but also Mayor George Moscone. Yet White would not silence Milk's legacy as the movement's first martyr, an outcome Milk himself had hoped for shortly before his murder: "If a bullet should enter my brain, let that bullet destroy every closet door."

D espite the clarity of his populist vision, his piercing as-
sessment of the socio-economic crisis confronting contemporary America, and his eloquent defense of personal liberties, Harvey Milk has been forgotten by the majority of
Americans. His is not a household name, invoking only blank
stares or the faintest glimmer of recognition. It is tragically
ironic that the notorious "twinkie defense" of his assassin [fel-
low San Francisco Supervisor Dan White, who claimed that
he was not responsible for his actions because of the effect on
him of the additives in his favorite junk food—Twinkies] is
better remembered by Americans than the mercurial Milk
himself. Those who do remember Milk remember him only
as a "minor" footnote in American history—the first openly
homosexual man to be popularly elevated into elective office
in the United States. To remember Milk solely for his sexual
orientation, however, is not only to misunderstand him, but his
concept of gay pride as well. Harvey Milk was one of the
most charismatic and pragmatic populists of the past half-
century, a man of remarkable organizational talent who never
compromised his vision of "a city of neighborhoods" nor
sought to hide his homosexuality.

Harvey Milk never intended to enter the political arena until he moved to San Francisco in 1972. Prior to Milk's arrival,
San Francisco's burgeoning homosexual population lacked a
sense of community, and consequently its political empowerment had been stunted. The city's homosexual intelligentsia—
weary of bearing the brutal brunt of police persecution and
public vilification—had organized several "educational" societies—designed to enlighten public opinion on the subject of
homosexuality in the early seventies. Since the idea of an
openly homosexual running for office in a city which still classified homosexuality as "a crime against nature"—punishable
by up to ten years in prison—seemed ludicrous to the homosexual intelligentsia, an integral component of these societies
were their political action committees. The homosexual political action committees (PACs) quickly succeeded in drawing
sympathetic "liberal friends" from the Democratic party to their

convocations, who—in return for their endorsement—promised to shield open homosexuals from officially sanctioned victimization. For the first time in American history, "mainstream" political figures treated their homosexual constituents with dignity and respect, actively courting their support.

The success of homosexual PACs was due in no small part to the fact that, "in this city of fewer than 700,000 people, approximately one out of every five adults and perhaps one out of every three or four voters was gay." At least half of the total homosexual population—like Milk himself—had moved to San Francisco between 1969 and 1977, bringing with them a bold assertiveness which had been sparked by the Stonewall riots of 1969 in New York City. Milk recognized the parallels between the growing gay enclaves and the traditional ethnic neighborhoods that made up the crazy-quilt fabric of San Francisco.

Many of these ethnic enclaves—such as the Irish and Italian sections of the city—had long since turned what had initially been a liability—their insularity—into a source of municipal power. It seemed only logical to Milk that the gay neighborhoods follow suit. If the homosexual vote was significant enough for "respectable" politicians to run the risk of alienating San Francisco's conservative voters by openly courting gay support, Milk reasoned, the homosexuals of San Francisco no longer needed to rely on "friends" for protection, but could rely on *themselves*.

> You see there is a major difference—and it remains a vital difference—between a friend and a gay person, a friend in office and a gay person in office. Gay people have been slandered nationwide . . . it's not just enough anymore just to have friends represent us, no matter how good that friend may be. . . . A gay official is needed not just for our protection, but to set an example for younger gays that says that the system works.

Milk's goal in asserting gay pride through political empowerment was not to force mainstream America to accept homosexuality, but to respect the homosexual's right to be homosexual, without governmental interference or hindrance. Milk fought not for the universal acceptance of homosexuality as "an alternate life-style," but for a universal acceptance of homosexuals as human beings, endowed by their creator with the same unalienable rights as their heterosexual counterparts. Whether his audience was sympathetic or hostile, Milk always depicted the struggle for gay rights as "the fight to preserve *your* democracy."

Like the black civil rights leaders of the fifties and sixties, whose example Milk exhorted gays nationwide to follow, Milk viewed *his* struggle to assert the "unalienable Rights" of homosexuals as the penultimate expression of the most cherished of American values: "Life, Liberty and the pursuit of Happiness." These basic American values were systematically denied homosexuals on the grounds of the Judeo-Christian abhorrence of homosexuality. Therefore, reason dictates that individual state and municipal governments had violated the Constitution's separation of church and state, when they codified homosexuality as "a crime against nature"—a naked assertion of a religious proscription over individual liberty.

The issue of sexuality, however, is seldom discussed on a rational plane, especially when the debate revolves around same-sex relations. As a result, hundreds of thousands of Americans were classified as "deviants" who, solely by virtue of their sexuality, were guilty of a felony which—according to the whims of local or state authorities—could lead to their prosecution, often resulting in public humiliation, institutionalization, and/or imprisonment. Such anti-gay statutes, many of which were relics either of the colonial or Victorian eras, were based upon the homophobic myths which form the basis of mainstream America's perception of homosexuality and homosexuals.

> The blacks did not win their rights by sitting quietly in the back of the bus. They got off! Gay people, we will not win our rights by staying quietly in our closets. . . . We are coming out! We are coming out to fight the lies, the myths, the distortions! We are coming out to tell the truth about gays!
> *[ellipse extant in text]*

SHATTERING THE INVISIBILITY OF GAY AMERICANS

Milk firmly believed that the only way for homosexuals to break down homophobia—"the last major dam of prejudice in this country"—was for homosexuals to make themselves visible: to step out of the closet, and into the consciousness of the nation. Whilst the images of the "drag queen" and "butch dyke" are firmly ensconced in the popular imagination, there are no "defining" homosexual traits; most homosexuals—male and female alike—are indistinguishable from heterosexuals. Unless an individual makes the conscious decision to overtly express his or her homosexuality, that individual remains a member of an invisible minority. This invisibility is magnified by the fact that the majority of homosexuals do not live openly in Greenwich Village or the Castro district of San Francisco, but instead live lives of silent suburban exile in a *society* that—despite the rhetoric of diversity—still dictates conformity. Thus, the majority of American homosexuals remain trapped behind walls of fear—the proverbial "closet"—rendering them utterly invisible to mainstream America. Milk argued that this invisibility only fosters homophobic stereotypes:

> Like every other group, we must be judged by our leaders and by those who are themselves gay, those who are visible. For invisible, we remain in limbo—a myth, a person with no parents, no brothers, no sisters, no friends who are straight, no important positions in employment. A tenth of our nation is supposedly composed of stereotypes and would-be seducers of children. But today, the black community is not judged by its friends, but by its black legislators and leaders. And we must give people the chance to judge us by our leaders and legislators. A gay person in office can set a tone, can command respect not only from the larger community, but from the young people in our own community who need both examples and hope.

Milk's entire political career was dedicated to shattering the silence of homosexual America and exposing the homophobic myths of heterosexual America. When he finally gained office—after three competitive but unsuccessful campaigns—Milk quickly transformed his public image, from "a gay politician" to a politician who "just happened" to be gay. By concentrating on implementing an aggressively populist agenda which encompassed the needs of *all* of San Francisco's minorities, Milk quickly dispelled the false issue of his sexual orientation. His passionate attention to detail and his dedication to improving the quality of life of *all* San Franciscans greatly widened his base of support. His adept handling of the media allowed him to transform the popular conception of who and what he was—"all over the country, they're reading about me," he told his aides several months after his election to the City Council, "and the story doesn't center on me being gay—it's just about a gay person who's doing his job."

MOBILIZING THE GAY COMMUNITY'S POLITICAL POWER

Milk's populism owed much to the unique composition of San Francisco. San Francisco had achieved its status as the largest Pacific seaport in America as a result of the century of successive waves of immigrants that followed the California gold rush. The city which arose from this constant influx was a crazy-quilt of ethnic neighborhoods—cities within the city. The homogeneous nature of each neighborhood's population served to preserve each particular neighborhood's ethnic identity through successive generations.

The characteristic component of San Francisco's most powerful ethnic neighborhoods was the merchants association. These associations were the source of the neighborhood's power, as they were an embodiment of the area's combined economic clout. Milk's first foray into politics had been to organize the homosexual community's businesses into a merchants association—the Castro Valley Association (CVA)—the gay community's first truly autonomous source of political power. As president of the CVA, Milk organized boycotts and pickets in support of many of the city's largest unions, gaining the gay community valuable and lasting allies. Much to the surprise of the city's professional politicians, Milk easily won the enthusiastic endorsement and material support of both the Teamsters and the Longshoremen's Unions when he first ran for Supervisor in 1973. Their support for Milk baffled the city's professional politicians who had traditionally relied upon these unions to muster blue collar vote on their behalf. Milk had simply learned the first rule of *realpolitik* [practical politics]—concrete results quickly eclipse most philosophical/moral qualms.

Harvey Milk was not a professional politician—he was the quintessential populist maverick. He owed no allegiance to any party or platform, leaving him free to follow the dictates of common sense, not dogma. This independence freed him from the compromising intrigues of inter-party politics, as well, allowing him to be ruled by his conscience rather than the accumulated debt traditional politicians owe special interest groups. Milk's populism stemmed from an absolute faith in the Jeffersonian principles of American democracy as outlined in the Declaration of Independence and in the inviolable sanctity of the Constitution.

The sole safeguard of individual rights, Milk fervently believed, is individual participation in the political process. As an open homosexual, Milk knew all too well that whoever holds the reins of power, dictates the limits of individual liberty. Milk perceived political parties—which he invariably referred to as "machines"—as the most pernicious threat to democracy. "Machines operate on oil and grease; they're dirty, dehumanizing, and too often unresponsive to any needs but those of the operator." The professional politician, therefore, was the representative not of the people, but of the special interests to which he had mortgaged his campaign.

OFFERING HOPE THROUGH POLITICS

During the sixties and seventies, a steadily increasing number of San Francisco's industries fled the city, opting to build new plants in the suburbs, rather than overhaul their aging and antiquated inner-city facilities. This urban flight eroded the city's poorer neighborhoods, whose blue-collar residents—mostly blacks and Hispanics who had relied on the plants for their livelihood—could not afford to follow their jobs to the suburbs. Instead of offering business incentives to remain in San Francisco, the city's civil administration—whose campaign had been heavily backed by developers, construction unions, and real estate concerns—launched an aggressive "urban renewal" campaign, which led to the razing of large segments of San Francisco's poorer ethnic neighborhoods to make room for office complexes and a mass transit system designed to lure tourists and corporate headquarters to the city.

The fruits of the machine's short-sighted "urban renewal" policy, was a shimmering skyline which was invaded daily by hordes of suburban-dwelling white-collar workers. At night, the skyline lay cold and vacant in the moonlight—its serene sterility obliterating the memory of the once vibrant neighborhood upon which it stood. The sterility of the skyline, however, was deceptive. "The scar that's left isn't just the empty office building or the now-vacant lot," Milk warned, "it's the worker who can no longer provide for his family, the teenager who suddenly awakens from the American Dream to find that all the jobs have gone south for the duration." The city had been mutilated by the machine; its wounds left to fester, as the inner-city neighborhoods crumbled, and the crime rate soared. "You see the empty buildings [where businesses used to be], but you don't see the hopelessness, the loss of pride, the anger," warned Milk.

Milk passionately believed that the "true function of politics is not just to pass laws, but to give hope." If the problems of the cities are not addressed, he warned, America's cities will plunge headlong into "the real abyss that lies not too far ahead, when a disappointed people lose their hope forever. When that happens, everything we cherish will be lost." The machine had betrayed the inner city, selling it out to "carpet-baggers who have fled to the suburbs," leaving behind omnipresent "fire hazards" in every inner-city neighborhood regardless of ethnicity. Milk viewed American cities as smoldering tinderboxes, which—unless defused, from the inside out—would continue to violently erupt, until the entire urban infrastructure of America was consumed by flames of rage.

A VOICE FOR ALL PEOPLE AGAINST THE "MACHINE"

In his campaign speeches of 1973–1977, Milk outlined his plans to bridge the deepening divide between the haves and the have-nots which "machines" across the country were creating. The core of Milk's populism was the simple belief that "the American Dream starts with the neighborhoods—if we wish to rebuild our cities, we must first rebuild our neighborhoods." The city could only be saved by the industry of its residents, Milk maintained, not "governmental charity." Rather than "face the problems it's created," and taking "responsibility for the problems it's ignored," the machine sought to bribe the urban poor with welfare programs. Instead of empowering the urban poor, these programs had actually trapped them in "concrete jungles," caged within a vicious cycle of dependence. In order to break this dependence, Milk maintained, the neighborhoods must firmly grasp the reins of power, in order to lead the city "down the route no major city has ever tried":

> that is the route that has little room for political payoffs and deals; that is the route that leaves little in the way of power politics; that is the route of making a city an exciting place for *all* to live: not just an exciting place for a few to live! A place for the individual and individual rights. There is no political gain in this nonmonied route and, thus you do not find people with high political ambitions leading this way. There are no statistics to quote—no miles of highways built to brag about, no statistics of giant buildings built under your administration. What you have instead is a city that breathes, one that is alive, where the people are more important than highways.

By reprioritizing government spending, Milk believed, the neighborhoods could begin the process of rebuilding the city from within, by utilizing the resources which the machine had squandered. Simply by mandating that all city employees must be residents of the city, the neighborhoods would have taken a giant step forward, Milk argued. From a fiscal standpoint, it made no sense to do otherwise, since city employees are paid with the tax revenues the city has raised from its residents. If the employee lives in the city, the money he is paid does not leave the city, but is recycled within the neighborhoods. Furthermore, exclusively employing residents of the city would ensure each distinct neighborhood that its policemen, firemen, ambulance drivers, etc., spoke the same language as it did, shared its values, understood the subtle nuances of its culture, and respected its way of life.

MILK'S LEGACY

The city could not afford to do otherwise, Milk warned:

> Unfortunately for those who would like to flee them, the problems of the cities don't stop at the city limits. There are no moats around our cities that keep the problems in. What happens in New York or San Francisco will eventually happen in San Jose. It's just a matter of time. And like the flu, it usually gets worse the further it travels. Our cities must not be abandoned. They're worth fighting for, not just by those who live in them, but by industry, commerce, unions, everyone. Not alone because they represent the past, but because they also represent the future. Your children will live there and hopefully, so will your grand-children.

"You can't run a city by people who don't live there," Milk warned America, "any more than you can have an effective police force made up of people who don't live there. In either case, what you've got is an occupying army."

Harvey Milk lent the power of his eloquent voice not only to the voiceless invisible minority, but to all minorities, whose voices are often lost in the gale winds of conformity that sweep the American cultural landscape. Milk often said that all he ever sought was "to open up a dialogue that involves all of us." Tragically, his assassin's bullet not only quelled his voice, but his populist vision as well. The machines ground on and the apocalyptic cycle of inner-city despair against which he battled has repeated itself in Homedale and South Central Los Angeles.

> Industry and business has made our country the greatest military and economic power in the world. Now I think it's time to look at our future with a realistic eye. I don't think the American Dream necessarily includes two cars in every garage and a disposal in every kitchen. What it does need is an educational system with incentives. To spend twelve years at school—almost a fifth of your life without a job at the other end is meaningless. Every ghetto child has the right to ask: Education for what?

Until his voice is resuscitated, his piercing question will remain unanswered.

The Political Necessities of a Gay Liberation Movement

MICHAEL DENNENY

Following the political actions of the 1960s and 1970s, Michael Denneny felt the gay community's goals needed to be reassessed in order to focus the movement's growing activities. While he acknowledges that his reflections are those of a gay man, and therefore may be of little or no use to lesbians, bisexuals, or transgenders, he believes that his propositions for change will benefit the entire movement: "[I]f we want to live in the world and not in the closet, we must create that world ourselves on every level."

Denneny is the author of *Lovers: The Story of Two Men* and one of the founders of *Christopher Street* magazine.

"Only within the framework
of a people can a man
live as a man without exhausting
himself." (Hannah Arendt [political theorist])

If society tries to destroy us by first isolating us, it follows that what is necessary to fight back is not only defiance but the acknowledgment of a community and the construction of a world. Individual defiance may lead to heroism—as we can see in the cases of [the writers] Quentin Crisp and Jean Genet—but, while we should honor our heroes, the cost is too high. Few individuals have the integrity or the energy to sus-

tain the violence to the soul and the consequent psychological deformations that heroism entails.

The further construction and consolidation of the gay
ghetto is an immediate and necessary political objective. The
singularity of the gay situation makes this "ghetto" unique,
generating perplexities we have barely begun to address and
rendering parallels to the experience of other groups dubious
at best. But this should not obscure the fact that *ghetto* is another
word for *world* and that *coming out* means asserting our right to
appear in the world as who we are. As Walter Lippmann observed (if not practiced): "Man must be at peace with the
sources of his life. If he is ashamed of them, if he is at war with
them, they will haunt him forever. They will rob him of the
basis of assurance, will leave him an interloper in the world."

From the blacks and the colonized we can learn much about
the pain of being interlopers in the world, "invisible men," but
we should also learn that if we want to live in the world and
not in the closet, we must create that world ourselves on every
level. It will not be handed to us on a silver platter. We need to
create networks of friendships, love relationships, public places
and institutions, neighborhoods, art, and literature. A gay culture is a political necessity for our survival.

DEMANDING THE FREEDOM SIMPLY TO BE

> Gay politics (using politics in
> its narrow meaning) is a
> politics of pure principle.

For us there is no "social question." We are not asking for a
bigger slice of the pie but for justice. We do not require social
programs, jobs, day-care centers, educational and professional
quotas, or any of the other legitimate demands of previously
exploited minority groups. Our demands will not cost the body
politic one cent. We demand only the freedom to be who we
are. The fact that this demand, which takes away nothing from
anyone else, is met with such obstinate resistance is a notewor-
thy indication of how deep-seated is the hostility against us.

On the other hand, we could expect that gay politics has its best chance in countries that are constitutional republics, where the belief that justice is the ultimate source of authority and legitimacy for the government gives us a powerful lever against the prejudice of society. It seems to me no accident that gay politics and gay culture have arisen first and most strongly in the United States. This is the only "nation" I know of that was brought into being by dissidents; whatever revisionist history may teach us are the facts of the case, the enormous authority the image of the Pilgrims and the Founding Fathers has for this country should not be underestimated. It often seems that non-American observers simply cannot understand our feeling that *as Americans* it is our *right* to be faggots if we choose—or as historian and lesbian novelist Noretta Koertge puts it: "Being American means being able to paint my mailbox purple if I want." Invoking the ultimate principles—if not realities—of this country is one of our most promising tactics, and should be explored and emphasized.

> We have *no natural allies*
> and therefore cannot rely on
> the assistance of any group.

We have only tactical allies—people who do not want barbarous things done to us because they fear the same things may someday be done to them. Tactical allies come into being when there is a perceived convergence of self-interest between two groups. One can accomplish much in politics with tactical allies, as witness the long alliance between blacks and Jews, but there are limits that emerge when the group-interests diverge, as witness the split between blacks and Jews over school decentralization in New York City.

A natural ally would be someone who is happy we are here, rather than someone who is unhappy at the way we are being treated. It would seem that the most we can expect, at least in the immediate future, is a tolerance based on decency. No one, no matter how decent, seems glad that gays exist, even when they may be enjoying works inspired by our sensibility. As far as I can see, even our best straight friends will never be thankful that we are gay in the way we ourselves (in our better moments) are thankful we are gay. This is nothing to get maudlin over. It does, however, sometimes seem to limit communication—the sharing that is the essence of friendship—with straights. It is a rare straight friend to whom one can say, "I'm so glad I'm gay because otherwise I never would have gotten the chance to love Ernie," and not draw a blank, if not bewildered and uncomfortable, reaction. It is understandable that they do not see it as something to celebrate—but we should.

On the personal level, it is generally unlikely that one's straight family or friends will easily learn genuine acceptance; luckily it would appear that they can, notwithstanding, often learn love. For our part, the paranoia that this situation tends naturally to generate should be rigorously controlled.

RECOGNIZING OUR ENEMIES

Our political enemies are
of two kinds:
those who want us not to exist
and those who want us not to appear.

Those who want us not to exist are the well-known, old-fashioned bigots, who would stamp us out, apply shock therapy or terroristic behavior modification, cordon us off and separate us from society, and ultimately try to kill us as the Nazis did. Fortunately these bigots are also a threat to many other segments of society and a number of tactical allies can be mobilized in the fight against them. Bigots are essentially bullies, and this bullying impulse seems to be exacerbated to the point of massacre by the lack of resistance. This suggests that the best response to them is probably a violent one: unchecked aggression seems to feed on itself and simply pick up velocity, like one of [King] Lear's rages. I suspect that when epithets are hurled at one in the street, it is best to shout epithets back; trying to ignore them with dignity or responding with overt fear seems only to intensify the hostility. Although

I am open to correction on this, I have the feeling that the *safest* response to physical assault is fighting back; the bruises one may incur seem to me preferable to the corrosive rage that follows from helplessness, and I suspect they might avoid a truly dangerous stomping. In short, bullies become worse bullies when they are unchecked and the cost of resistance is probably worth it in the long run.

Those who want us not to appear are more subtle and probably more dangerous, since it is harder to mobilize tactical allies against them. This seemed to me the most significant aspect of the Anita Bryant phenomenon [in 1977]. By carefully explaining that she was only against overt gay behavior—the "flaunting" of our life-style and the consequent "recruitment"—she managed to seem reasonable to a large segment of the public; by disavowing any McCarthy-type witch hunt, she managed to avoid tripping the wire that would have sent large parts of the Jewish community of Miami onto red alert. The difficulty of countering these people successfully is rooted in the fact that we *can* pass, a characteristic that distinguishes us from other minority groups, and is further compounded by the fact that when you come right down to it *everyone* would be more comfortable if we remained in the closet except ourselves.

These matters require much more consideration than we have yet given them. We cannot rely forever on the stupidity of our opponents—for instance, in the overreaching language of the [1978] Briggs Initiative in California [to permit the firing of gay teachers], which led to its rejection for First Amendment reasons that were so obvious they even penetrated the mind of the public. It is urgent to give tactical and strategic thought to these matters—always keeping in mind the fact that in their heart of hearts the overwhelming majority of the American people would prefer us back in the closet. Our only hope is to make it clear that that would be so costly that they will not be willing to pay the price.

"The only remedy
for powerlessness is power."
(Charles Ortleb)

Economic exploitation, one of the great nineteenth-century themes of political discourse, has largely been replaced in our own day by the discussion of oppression. Exploitation means basically that someone is stealing from you; oppression is essentially a matter of invisibility, of feeling weightless and insubstantial, without voice or impact in the world. Blacks, the colonized, women, and gays all share this experience of being a ghost in their own country, the disorienting alienation of feeling they are not actually there. This psychological experience is the subjective correlate to the objective fact of powerlessness.

It is odd that the desire for power has for many an unpleasant aura about it, for powerlessness is a true crime against the human spirit and undercuts the possibility of justice among people. In his *Inquiry Concerning the Principles of Morals*, David Hume lays this out quite clearly, albeit without being aware of it, when he speculates that "were there a species intermingled with men which, though rational, were possessed of such inferior strength, both of body and mind, that they were incapable of all resistance and could never, upon the highest provocation, make us feel the effects of their resentment, the necessary consequence, I think, is that we ... should not, properly speaking, lie under any restraint of justice with regard to them. ... Our intercourse with them could not be called society, which supposes a degree of equality, but absolute command on the one side, and servile obedience on the other. ... Our permission is the only tenure by which they hold their possessions, our compassion and kindness the only check by which they [sic] curb our lawless will ... the restraints of justice ... would never have place in so unequal a confederacy."

Well, we know there are such "creatures intermingled with men"—women first of all, and the colonized races, as well as homosexuals, Jews, and mental patients. It is truly strange that this philosopher, who seems to think he is idly speculating, was quite clearly laying out the premises of the power structure that at that very moment was subjugating so many groups of people. And with two centuries of hindsight, it should be clear to all of us just how effective their "compassion and kindness" is as a check against their "lawless will." If we have to rely on "the laws of humanity" to convince them "to give gentle usage to these creatures," we will stay precisely where we have been, under their heel being stomped on.

I do not pretend to understand the origin and mechanics of this strange social system in which we live. But it seems to me it should be abundantly clear to even the dimmest wit that without power you will not get justice. How anybody could rely on "compassion and kindness" after looking around at the world we live in is beyond me. "Moderate" gays who think we can achieve tolerance by respectability seem to me willfully ignorant of our own history, as well as the history of other oppressed groups. They are the court Jews of our time, however good their subjective intentions.

Straights who object to our daily increasing visibility are basically objecting to the assertion of power implicit in that phenomenon. They would prefer that we continue to rely on their "compassion and kindness" and correctly sense that our refusal to do so directly insults them. With their record on the matter it is hard to imagine why they are surprised. In fact, our extraordinary explosion into visibility, the spontaneous and visible assertion of our sexual identity that constitutes the clone look is politically valuable. Not only are we more visible to each other, we are more visible to them. Of course, one would naturally expect a backlash at this point; it is virtually unknown in history for any group to give up power over any other without a struggle. . . .

Gay liberation has no chance in hell of liberating society sexually. (The reverse argument is, of course, valid, if tautological; the sexual liberation of society would indeed entail the liberation of gays. The problem is only: what will cause the sexual liberation of society, who will bring this about? You see how one could fall into thinking about the agent or carrier of historical change.) Gay liberation will not be the carrier of the revolutionary idea if for no other reason than the fact that by "revolutionary idea" is meant the revaluation of all values, and values are not "things" that can be "carried" like shoulder bags or diseases. A discussion of the nature of value, however, would take us too far afield.

If gay liberation is not going to liberate society, has it any meaning beyond that of promoting the self-interests of the individuals who make up this particular group? (I hasten to add that defending and promoting the self-interest of any oppressed group is in itself totally justifiable.) I think the answer is affirmative, if somewhat speculative at this point.

It has been known for well over a century now that something is drastically wrong with our culture; our values seem to be working in reverse. Western civilization looks more and more like the sorcerer's apprentice: it has unleashed powers that threaten to overwhelm it. Nihilism is the name usually applied to this phenomenon. Our values have turned against us and threaten devastation if not extinction. This sounds rhetorical. It is not. It is a simple description of the current state of affairs, as a moment's uncomfortable reflection on the Holocaust, the threat of nuclear annihilation, the consequences of pollution and irreversible ecological intervention, genetic engineering, or a dozen other phenomena reported daily in the papers, makes quite clear. We need a revaluation of all our values, but how can this be accomplished if there is no Archimedian point [immutable foundation] on which to stand? If the salt has lost its savor, wherewith shall it be salted?

I suggest that the complex, subtle, everyday transformation of values that we gays have been engaged in for the last ten years, the self-renewal that constitutes gay liberation, is a creative response to the viciously negative values of our culture. As such, it would be *a part* of that urgently necessary revaluation of all values and could serve not as a historical catalyst that will save anybody else but as an example of what is necessary and as a welcome ally to those already engaged by this challenge. In the struggle for gay liberation we come home to ourselves and our world and take our place among the ranks of decent and responsible people everywhere who stand together at this decisive moment in humanity's career on the planet.

CHAPTER 3

THE STRUGGLE FOR SURVIVAL

AMERICAN
SOCIAL
MOVEMENTS

Ethical Propaganda? Using Advertising to Combat Homophobia

MARSHALL KIRK AND HUNTER MADSEN

This excerpt is taken from *After the Ball: How America Will Conquer Its Fear and Hatred of Gays in the '90s.* An examination of the contemporary gay rights movement, it was written by Marshall Kirk, a neuropsychiatry researcher, logician, and poet, in collaboration with Hunter Madsen, a public communications expert who guided the first national advertising effort to promote positive images of gays and lesbians.

In the following selection, the authors explore how manipulating the mainstream press can become a tool to combat homophobia in the United States. After desensitizing the public by flooding the media with gay-related images and advertising, conversion can then occur, the authors speculate, by taking "the bigot's good feelings about all-right guys, and attach[ing] them to the label 'gay,' either weakening or, eventually, replacing his bad feelings toward the label and the prior stereotype."

The authors reject possible objections to their proposal—for example, that projecting only images of "normal-looking" gays inadequately reflects the entire community—by affirming that the end in this case—combating homophobia—justifies the means.

Desensitization aims at lowering the intensity of antigay emotional reactions to a level approximating sheer indifference; Jamming attempts to blockade or counteract the re-

Marshall Kirk and Hunter Madsen, *After the Ball: How America Will Conquer Its Fear and Hatred of Gays in the '90s.* New York: Doubleday, 1989. Copyright © 1989 by Marshall Kirk and Hunter Madsen. Reproduced by permission of Doubleday, a division of Random House, Inc.

warding 'pride in prejudice' (peace, Jane Austen!) by attaching to homohatred a pre-existing, and punishing, sense of shame in being a bigot, a horse's ass, and a beater and murderer. Both Desensitization and Jamming, though extremely useful, are mere preludes to our highest—though necessarily very long-range—goal, which is Conversion.

It isn't enough that antigay bigots should become confused about us, or even indifferent to us—we are safest, in the long run, if we can actually make them like us. Conversion aims at just this.

Please don't confuse *Con*version with political *Sub*version. The word 'subversion' has a nasty ring, of which the American people are inordinately afraid—and on their guard against. Yet, ironically, by Conversion we actually mean something far more profoundly threatening to the American Way of Life, without which no truly sweeping social change can occur. We mean conversion of the average American's emotions, mind, and will, through a planned psychological attack, in the form of propaganda fed to the nation via the media. We mean 'subverting' the mechanism of prejudice to our own ends—using the very processes that made America hate us to turn their hatred into warm regard—whether they like it or not.

Put briefly, if Desensitization lets the watch run down, and Jamming throws sand in the works, Conversion reverses the spring so that the hands run backward.

CREATING AN APPEALING STEREOTYPE

Conversion makes use of Associative Conditioning [the psychological process whereby when two things are repeatedly juxtaposed, one's feelings about one thing are transferred to the other thing], much as Jamming does—indeed, in practice the two processes overlap—but far more ambitiously. In Conversion, the bigot, who holds a very negative stereotypic picture, is repeatedly exposed to literal picture/label pairs, in magazines, and on billboards and TV, of gays—explicitly labeled as such!—who not only don't look like his picture of a homosexual, but are carefully selected to look either like the bigot

Changing Beliefs Through a Gay Advertising Campaign

Before Conversion	After Conversion
1. Gays don't warrant or deserve much attention from straights.	*Gays are a valuable part of American society: we should be familiar with their nature, culture, news, and heroes.*
2. Gays are few in number; I don't know any gays.	*Gays constitute a large minority of our society; and some of my friends/family are gay.*
3. Gays are easy to spot.	*They are not: most of them look just like anyone else.*
4. Gays become gay because of sin, insanity, and seduction.	*Sexual feelings are not really chosen by anybody: homosexuality is just as healthy and natural for some persons as heterosexuality is for others.*
5. Gays are kinky sex addicts.	*The sex and love lives of most gays and straights today are both similar and conventional.*
6. Gays are unproductive, untrustworthy members of society.	*Gays are hardworking, patriotic Americans.*
7. Gays are suicidally unhappy.	*Gays would be as happy as anyone else, if we'd just treat them fairly.*

Marshall Kirk and Hunter Madsen, "The Waging Peace Agenda for Change Among Straights," *After the Ball: How America Will Conquer Its Fear and Hatred of Gays in the '90s.* New York: Doubleday, 1989, p. 107.

and his friends, or like any one of his other stereotypes of all-right guys—the kind of people he already likes and admires. This image must, of necessity, be carefully tailored to be free of absolutely every element of the widely held stereotypes of how 'faggots' look, dress, and sound. He—or she—must not be too well or fashionably dressed; must not be too hand-some—that is, mustn't look like a model—or well groomed. The image must be that of an icon of normality—a good be-ginning would be to take a long look at Coors beer and Three Musketeers candy commercials. Subsequent ads can branch out from that solid basis to include really adorable, athletic teen-agers, kindly grandmothers, avuncular policemen, *ad infinitum*.

The objection will be raised—and raised, and raised—that we would 'Uncle Tommify' the gay community; that we are exchanging one false stereotype for another equally false; that our ads are lies; that that is *not* how *all* gays actually look; that gays know it, and bigots know it. Yes, of course—we know it, too. But it makes no difference that the ads are lies; not to us, because we're using them to ethically good effect, to counter negative stereotypes that are every bit as much lies, and far more wicked ones; not to bigots, because the ads will have their effect on them whether they believe them or not.

When a bigot is presented with an image of the sort of person of whom he already has a positive stereotype, he ex-periences an involuntary rush of positive emotion, of good feeling; he's been conditioned to experience it. But, here, the good picture has the bad label—gay! (The ad may say some-thing rather like 'Beauregard Smith—beer drinker, Good Ole Boy, pillar of the community, 100% American, and gay as a mongoose.') The bigot will feel two incompatible emotions: a good response to the picture, a bad response to the label. At worst, the two will cancel one another, and we will have successfully Jammed, as above. At best, Associative Condi-tioning will, to however small an extent, transfer the positive emotion associated with the picture to the label itself, not immediately replacing the negative response, but definitely weakening it.

A Picture Is Worth a Thousand Conversions

You may wonder why the transfer wouldn't proceed in the opposite direction. The reason is simple: pictures are stronger than words and evoke emotional responses more powerfully. The bigot is presented with an *actual* picture; its label will evoke in his mind his own stereotypic picture, but what he sees in his mind's eye will be weaker than what he actually sees in front of him with the eyes in his face. The more carefully selected the advertised image is to reflect his ideal of the sort of person who just couldn't be gay, the more effective it will be. Moreover, he will, by virtue of logical necessity, see the positive picture in the ad *before* it can arouse his negative 'picture,' and first impressions have an advantage over second.

In Conversion, we mimic the natural process of stereotype-learning, with the following effect: we take the bigot's good feelings about all-right guys, and attach them to the label 'gay,' either weakening or, eventually, replacing his bad feelings toward the label and the prior stereotype.

Understanding Direct Emotional Modeling [the inborn tendency of human beings to feel what they perceive others to be feeling], you'll readily foresee its application to Conversion: whereas in Jamming the target is shown a bigot being rejected by his crowd for his prejudice against gays, in Conversion the target is shown his crowd actually associating with gays in good fellowship. Once again, it's very difficult for the average person, who, by nature and training, almost invariably feels what he sees his fellows feeling, not to respond in this knee-jerk fashion to a sufficiently calculated advertisement. In a way, most advertisement is founded upon an answer of Yes, definitely! to Mother's sarcastic question: I suppose if all the other kids jumped off a bridge and killed themselves, you would, too?

The Gay Community Must Mobilize Against AIDS

LARRY KRAMER

Larry Kramer delivered the following speech at the Gay and Lesbian Community Center in New York on March 10, 1987. His contempt for the profit-driven pharmaceutical and insurance industries, his despair for the thousands of men who were dead and dying of AIDS, and his disillusionment with what he perceived as more passive organizations such as Gay Men's Health Crisis (GMHC) inspired the creation of ACT UP—the AIDS Coalition to Unleash Power. This ad hoc community protest group exerted enormous influence over the development of treatments, the release of more effective drugs, and the funding of community services. Today, though Kramer is no longer an active member, ACT UP continues its fight against AIDS.

O n March 14th, 1983, almost four years ago to this date, I wrote an article in the *New York Native*. There were at that time 1,112 cases of AIDS nationwide. My article was entitled "1,112 and Counting," and through the courtesy of *Native* publisher Chuck Ortleb, it was reprinted in seventeen additional gay newspapers across the country. Here are a few of the opening sentences from this article:

"If this article doesn't scare the shit out of you, we're in real trouble. If this article doesn't rouse you to anger, fury, rage, and action, gay men may have no future on this earth. Our continued existence depends on just how angry you can get. . . . I repeat: Our continued existence as gay men upon the face of this earth is at stake. Unless we fight for our lives, we shall die. In all the history of homosexuality we have never before been so close to death and extinction."

When I wrote that, four years ago, there were 1,112 cases of AIDS nationwide. There are now officially—and we all know how officials count—32,000 with 10,000 of these in New York.

We have not yet even begun to live through the true horror. As it has been explained to me, the people who have become ill so far got ill early; the average incubation period is now thought to be five and one-half years, and the real tidal wave is yet to come: people who got infected starting in 1981. You had sex in 1981. I did, too. And after.

Last week, I had seven friends who were diagnosed. In one week. That's the most in the shortest period that's happened to me.

THE TERRIFYING MORTALITY RATE

I would like everyone from this right-hand side aisle, all the way to the left-hand side of the room—would you stand up for a minute, please? [They do so.] At the rate we are going, you could be dead in less than five years. Two-thirds of this room could be dead in less than five years. Please sit down.

Let me rephrase my *Native* article of 1983. If my speech tonight doesn't scare the shit out of you, we're in real trouble. If what you're hearing doesn't rouse you to anger, fury, rage, and action, gay men will have no future here on earth. How long does it take before you get angry and fight back?

I sometimes think we have a death wish. I think we must want to die. I have never been able to understand why for six long years we have sat back and let ourselves literally be knocked off man by man—without fighting back. I have heard of denial, but this is more than denial; it *is* a death wish.

I don't want to die. I cannot believe that you *want* to die.

But what are we doing, *really*, to save our own lives?

Two-thirds of you—I should say of *us*, because I am in this, too—could be dead within five years. Two-thirds of this room could be dead within five years.

What does it take for us to take responsibility for our own lives? Because we are *not*—we are not taking responsibility for our own lives.

HOPE IN THE HEART OF TEXAS

I want to talk about a few specific things.

I've just come back from Houston. My play *The Normal Heart* was done at the Alley Theatre there. I did not want to go to see it, but a very insistent woman who works with AIDS patients there would not take no for an answer. Thus I had the opportunity and the great privilege to visit our country's first AIDS hospital, which is called the Institute for Immunological Disorders. I've finally discovered the place I want to go to if I get sick.

You know how the topic of conversation in New York always turns to: Where would you go if you got sick? Which hospital? Which doctor? Quite frankly, I don't want to go to *any* hospital in New York. And I don't want to go to most of the doctors. They pooh-pooh everything new that comes along; they don't know anything about any new drug or treatment. They don't want to know. They throw you into the hospital, give you a grotesquely expensive workup, pump you full of some old drug that they've heard about from another doctor, and your insurance company pays for it, if you're lucky enough to have insurance. These doctors won't fight for anything, they won't go up against the Food and Drug Administration (FDA); they don't want to hear about any new theories or ideas. Why are they always so negative about everything? These doctors are making a fucking fortune out of us. They ridicule anything new that comes along, without even trying it. The horror stories emanating from almost every hospital in this city, with the possible exception of New York University (NYU), are just grotesque—all the way from an attempted murder of an AIDS patient at a New York hospital to a friend of mine who lay in the emergency room at

St. Vincent's for seventeen hours, just last week, before anyone looked at him. No, I don't want to go to any hospital or any doctor in New York.

The Institute for Immunological Disorders is run by Dr. Peter Mansell, who is one of the top AIDS doctors in America. It has space for 150 patients. There are only sixteen patients there. This most wonderful AIDS hospital in the world—you probably don't even know about it; some of you are hearing about it for the first time. How can it happen that it only has sixteen patients? Only in America.

HOPE DENIED

I'm going to tell you—it's not explicitly germane to us, but it is interesting—Texas is the only state in this country where if you don't have insurance, where if you're indigent, the state will not reimburse you or a hospital for the cost of your care. Most of those with AIDS in Houston don't have any insurance. They can't afford to go to Dr. Mansell's hospital. Mansell treats 150 patients every week, as outpatients, for free. Dr. Mansell's hospital, which is owned by a for-profit corporation, is losing a great deal of money. This hospital must not be allowed to die.

Dr. Mansell has found out some very interesting things. He has found out that 90 percent of all AIDS problems are better treated at home, and this includes home treatment for pneumocystis carinii pneumonia (PCP). He has found that he can treat patients for two-thirds less than it costs anywhere else—an average of $11,000 vs. $33,000. He has found that the average length of hospital stay of his patients is ten days, versus thirty days anywhere else. The hitch, of course, is that no insurance policy covers outpatient care. The very insurance companies that are threatening to take away our insurance because we cost them too much won't pay for cheaper treatment. That doesn't make much sense, does it?

But the real horror stories that Dr. Mansell told me have to do with drugs and the FDA. Dr. Mansell has five drugs waiting to be tested. I never heard of four of them. He tells me that each has been shown to prove as promising as [the drug] AZT was when it was approved. Each has passed what are called Phase One Safety Trials, which show them to lack noticeable side effects. The drugs are called Ampligen, Glucan, DTC, AS 101, and MTP-PE (for Kaposi's sarcoma). He cannot get near the FDA. When one of the top AIDS doctors in the United States can't get protocols through the FDA, we're in big trouble. He showed me the protocols that he submits, and he showed me how they're sent back—the FDA asking for one sentence rewritten, three words revised—nothing substantial—each change causing a delay of six to eight months. Ampligen is a drug that has been around for a long time. Concerned citizens of Houston have formed a foundation and bought $250,000 worth of Ampligen, so neither the hospital nor the government had to pay for it—and the drug remains unused and untested because of FDA quibbling.

PROFIT, NOT COMPASSION, DETERMINES THE RACE FOR A CURE

You know—each step of this horror story that we live through, we come up against an even bigger brick wall. First it was the city, then the state, then the Centers for Disease Control (CDC), then the National Institutes of Health (NIH). Now it's the FDA. Ann Fettner wrote last week in the *Village Voice* about the FDA: "It is a bureaucratic mess, they aren't even computerized, things 'are likely to get stuck in the mailroom,' says Duke University economist Henry Grabowski—which means that much of our pharmaceutical talent diddles with refinements of approved drugs while many that are desperately needed are put on hold." A new drug can easily take ten years to satisfy FDA approval. Ten years! Two-thirds of us could be dead in less than five years.

In 1980 the then head of the FDA said, "Ribavirin is probably the most important product discovered during the intensive search for antiviral agents." It's 1987 and we still can't get it. Fettner says, "It's astonishing that ribavirin wasn't chosen before AZT." Leading researchers I have talked to explain this one way: The FDA doesn't like the difficult, obstreperous head of ICN Pharmaceuticals, which manufactures ribavirin, while Burroughs Wellcome, which makes AZT, is smooth, politically savvy, with strong public relations (PR) people. The fast introduction of AZT was described to me in one word by a leading doctor: "Greed." He thinks little of AZT, refers to it as "yesterday's drug, that Burroughs Wellcome is trying to make their fortune out of before it's too late. I have too many patients on it who are becoming transfusion-dependent." I have a few friends who seem to be doing well on it. I have some who aren't. It's certainly not our savior.

AL 721 isn't even a drug—it's a food! How dare the FDA refuse to get it into fast circulation when it has proved promising in Israel at their famous Weizmann Institute? Indeed, Praxis Pharmaceuticals, which holds the American rights to it, could put it out as a food; but they apparently are gambling for big bucks by waiting for FDA approval to put it out as a drug, which is going to take forever, because Praxis doesn't appear to have much experience in putting out drugs at all. Rumor has it, also, that Praxis has forbidden the Weizmann Institute and Israeli doctors from giving AL 721 to any non-Israelis who go to Israel to get it.

TREATMENT DELAYS ARE HASTENING OUR DEATHS

What's going on here? To quote Dr. Mansell: "The FDA makes me froth at the mouth." We have reached a brick wall. There is a fortune being tossed at AIDS, but it's not buying anything. To quote Dr. Mansell: "A lot of money, a lot of energy—and very little to show for it." He runs one of the NIH-designated AIDS treatment centers and he has a hospital with *sixteen* patients! And we have ten thousand cases in New York City. He has an empty hospital, and he is one of the smartest men in this epidemic. How can this country be so wasteful!

Another researcher: "The NIH is too slow and too determined to maintain central control. It is hugely bureaucratic, much like your own Gay Men's Health Crisis (GMHC) and other AIDS organizations have become." Not my words. Dr. Mansell again: "Many of the drugs that the NIH is testing have already proved useless and ineffective somewhere else. Why do they insist on testing them? Why do they refuse to test any of these new drugs that are brought to their attention?"

Let's talk about double-blind studies that we're forced to endure. Did you know that double-blind studies were not created originally for terminal illnesses? I never knew that. Did you know that? How dare they, then, make us endure double-blind studies? They are ludicrously inhumane when two-thirds of this room could be dead in less than five years.

Double-blind studies are also exceptionally foolish, because people with AIDS (PWAs) lie to get the drugs. I'd lie. Wouldn't you? If they told me what to say to get a promising treatment, I'd say it, whether it was true or not. I have friends who have forged their medical records, who have gone to medical libraries to learn the correct terminology to fill in the blanks. So all the results from all these double-blind studies aren't going to tell anyone a thing. We're willing to be guinea pigs, all of us. Give us the fucking drugs! Especially if Dr. Mansell has five drugs that he says may have fewer side effects than AZT.

MONEY, MONEY EVERYWHERE, BUT NO CURE IN SIGHT

Almost one billion dollars will be thrown at AIDS, and it's not buying anything that will save two-thirds of the people in this room. I just heard about a college on Long Island that's been awarded a $600,000 grant from the Centers for Disease Control—an organization I have come to loathe—to study AIDS stress on college students. I can tell them right now and save the government $600,000. I know what it's like to be stressed. So do you.

I called up the offices of our elected officials and asked them to send someone here tonight. New York Governor Mario Cuomo, New York Senator Alfonse D'Amato, New York Senator Patrick Moynihan, New York City Major Ed Koch. Every single one of them treated me as if I was ungrateful. "We have been on the front line of getting you your money," each one of them said. "Leave us alone. You got your money. What else do you want?" That was from Moynihan's office: "What else do you want? We got you your money." When I try to tell them that this money isn't working right, isn't buying us anything, isn't properly supervised—once again, they don't want to know. I find the offices of Moynihan and D'Amato particularly insensitive to gay issues. Our only friend in Congress, and he's getting real tired, is Ted Weiss [from New York]. And, of course, from Los Angeles, Henry Waxman.

So what are we going to do? Time and time again I have said—no one is going to do it for us but ourselves.

THE GAY COMMUNITY MUST COME TOGETHER TO FIGHT FOR OUR SURVIVAL

We have always been a particularly divisive community. We fight with each other too much, we're disorganized, we simply cannot get together. We've all insulted each other. I'm as much at fault in this as anyone.

I came back from Houston and I called people I haven't spoken to in many years. I called Paul Popham. Those of you who are familiar with the history of GMHC and with *The Normal Heart* will know of the fights that he and I had and the estrangement of what had once been an exceptionally close friendship. Paul is very ill now. He and I spoke for over an hour. It was as if it were the early days of GMHC again, and we were planning strategy of what had to be done. We talked not about the hurts that each had caused the other. He supported me in everything that I am saying to you tonight, and that I have been writing about in the *Native* in recent issues. He would be here tonight, except that he had chemotherapy today. He asked me to say some things to you. "Tell them we have to make gay people all over the country cooperate. Tell them we have to establish some way to cut through all the red tape. We have to find a way to make GMHC, the AIDS Action Council, and the other AIDS organizations stronger and more political."

We talked a lot about GMHC, the organization that represents so much of our joint lives. As you know, I have been very critical of GMHC recently, and wrote a rather stinging attack on them. Paul and I both feel that GMHC is the only AIDS game in town in this country, and, like it or not, they have to be made to act stronger in the areas of lobbying and advocacy. There are no other organizations with as much clout, with as much money, with as much staff. San Francisco's AIDS organizations still have not even put their pledged contributions into the AIDS Action Council, our joint lobbying effort in Washington, which is an appalling act on the part of San Francisco's gay community. "We have to shame them into their contributions," Paul said.

The people administering GMHC are running what amounts to a big corporation. We cannot fault them for running such a sound ship, such a fiscally sound ship.

But we desperately need leadership in this crisis. We desperately need a central voice and a central organization to which everything else can plug in and be coordinated through. There isn't anyone else. And in this area of centralized leadership, of vision, of seeing the larger picture and acting upon it, GMHC is tragically weak. It seems to have lost the sense of mission and urgency upon which it was founded—which Paul and I fought so hard to give it.

EXISTING GROUPS ARE TOO PASSIVE

In my recent article attacking them, I asked GMHC for very specific things: lobbying; an advocacy division; more public-relations people to get the word out; a change of their tax-exempt status to allow for increased political activities; fighting for drugs; more strong members put on their Board. I was promised everything. I couldn't believe it; it was too good to be true.

Two months later, precious little has been done. The tax-exempt status has been changed. A lobbyist has been identified for Albany. A *part-time* PR person is about to be hired. When I asked why they were not hiring a full-time PR person, *six* full-time PR persons, the excuse I was given was "We don't have a desk." Two-thirds of us are going to be dead in five years, and this rich organization is not hiring people to get the word out because they haven't got room for a desk. [Cries from the audience of "Shame, shame!"]

No advocacy plan has emerged from GMHC, despite the fact that we have been promised one for six months. Paul Popham himself told me that the "Mission Statement" that was prepared by GMHC's executives is one that he never would have accepted when he was president of the Board.

Today's front page of *The New York Times* has an article about two thousand Catholics marching through the halls of Albany today. On the front page of the *Times.* With their six bishops (including one whom we know to be gay). Two thousand Catholics and their bishops marching through the halls of government. That's advocacy! That's what GMHC has to plan and facilitate and encourage. That's what all of us have to do. Southern Methodist University gets on national television protesting something about their football team. Black people marched on Mayor Koch's apartment only days after Howard Beach [where a group of white people chased a black man onto a highway where he was struck and killed by a car]. Why are we so invisible, constantly and forever! What does it take to get a few thousand people to stage a march!

WE MUST MOBILIZE PROTESTS AND GOVERNMENT LOBBYING

Did you notice what got the most attention at the recent CDC conference in Atlanta? It was a bunch called the Lavender Hill Mob. They got more attention than anything else at that meeting. They protested. They yelled and screamed and demanded and were blissfully rude to all those arrogant epidemiologists who are ruining our lives.

We can no longer afford to operate in separate and individual cocoons. There cannot be a Lavender Hill Mob protesting without a Gay and Lesbian Alliance Against Defamation (GLAAD) mobilizing the media, without a National Gay and

Lesbian Task Force and AIDS Action Council lobbying in Washington, without a Human Rights Campaign Fund raising money, and without a GMHC and its leaders leading us. That's coordination. Without every organization working together, networking, we will get nowhere.

We must immediately rethink the structure of our community, and that is why I have invited you here tonight: to seek your input and advice, in the hope that we can come out of tonight with some definite and active ideas. Do we want to reactivate the old AIDS Network? Do we want to start a new organization devoted solely to political action?

I want to talk to you about power. We are all in awe of power, of those who have it, and we always bemoan the fact that we don't have it. Power is little pieces of paper on the floor. No one picks them up. Ten people walk by and no one picks up the piece of paper on the floor. The eleventh person walks by and is tired of looking at it, and so he bends down and picks it up. The next day he does the same thing. And soon he's in charge of picking up the paper. And he's got a lot of pieces of paper that he's picked up. Now—think of those pieces of paper as standing for responsibility. This man or woman who is picking up the pieces of paper is, by being responsible, acquiring more and more power. He doesn't necessarily want it, but he's tired of seeing the floor littered. All power is the willingness to accept responsibility. But we live in a city and a country where no one is willing to pick up pieces of paper. Where no one wants any responsibility.

IT'S TIME FOR US TO TAKE RESPONSIBILITY FOR OUR SURVIVAL

It's easy to criticize GMHC. It's easier to criticize, period. It's harder to do things. Every one of us here is capable of doing something. Of doing something strong. We have to go after the FDA—fast. That means coordinated protests, pickets, arrests. Are you ashamed to be arrested? I would like to acknowledge one of the most courageous men in this country, who is with us here tonight. He is so concerned about the proliferation of nuclear weapons that he gets arrested at the expense of his own career. He uses his name and his fame to help make this world a better place. Martin Sheen. Stand up, Martin. The best man at Martin's wedding, his oldest friend, died today, from AIDS.

Look at this article from the *San Francisco Chronicle,* written by openly gay journalist Randy Shilts (just about the only reporter and the only newspaper in this entire country covering AIDS with proper thoroughness and compassion). Look who is our friend: the Surgeon General, C. Everett Koop. A fundamentalist is our friend. Koop said, "We have to embarrass the administration into bringing the resources that are necessary to deal with this epidemic forcefully." He said a meeting has been arranged with the President [Ronald Reagan] several times, and several times this meeting has been canceled. His own Surgeon General is telling us that we have to embarrass the President to get some attention to AIDS. Why didn't any other paper across this country pick up this story? You sure didn't see it in *The New York Times.*

It's our fault, boys and girls. It's our fault. Two thousand Catholics can walk through the corridors of Albany. The American Foundation for AIDS Research has on its board Elizabeth Taylor, Warren Beatty, Leonard Bernstein, Woody Allen, Barbra Streisand, Michael Sovern (the president of Columbia University), a veritable *Who's Who;* why can't they get a meeting with the President—their former acting buddy? Why don't we think like that?

Well, until we all bend over and pick up all those little pieces of paper, I don't have to tell you what's going to happen.

Keeping the Faith:
Gay Activism in the
Catholic Church

TIM DLUGOS

For years, Tim Dlugos called himself "a Catholic with a sense of paradox." In 1968 he entered the Christian Brothers, a religious order of laymen in the Catholic Church, only to leave three years later—one month after he came out as a gay man. His struggle to balance his religion with his sexual orientation is not unique, nor is it in fact limited to gay laity. Gay clergy all across the nation must remain in the closet or risk shame, ridicule, and defrocking (to deprive clergy of the right to exercise the functions of their offices).

In the following selection, Dlugos profiles the New Ways Ministry, founded in 1971 as a forum for clergy to discuss their hopes and fears about being gay in the Catholic Church. One of the first such outlets for gay clergy, the ministry continues today as "a gay-positive ministry of advocacy and justice for lesbian and gay Catholics and reconciliation within the larger Christian and civil communities."

Dlugos is the author of *Entre Nous*, a poetry collection, and his articles and reviews have appeared in the *Washington Post Book World* and *Soho News* among others.

Jeannine Gramick takes a sip of iced tea. "Since 1971," she says, "we've seen a lot of changes in the church's attitude toward gay people that others haven't seen. I think that people in the church are getting ready to deal with it."

It is a hot afternoon. But Gramick is getting used to heat. She and her colleague, Robert Nugent, have taken a lot of it this year—from the Vatican's Sacred Congregation for Religious, from the Archdiocese of Washington, and from Catholic newspapers around the country. Gramick is a School Sister of Notre Dame; Nugent is a Salvatorian priest whose faculties to say mass in the Washington area have been suspended. Together they are New Ways Ministry, a self-described "ministry of reconciliation and social justice for Catholic gay persons, other sexual minorities, their families, friends, and the larger Catholic community."

The apartment where they work, in Mount Rainier, Maryland, is part of a dusty collection of low-rises just across the D.C. line from Catholic University, an area riddled with dozens of communities of sisters, priests, and brothers. (As a novice in the Christian Brothers, I passed through the neighborhood every morning on my way to theology class at my order's now-defunct Washington house of studies.) Their working space is small but cheery: two old wooden desks next to the living-room window; a portable typewriter; a framed poster of Picasso's *Don Quixote* on the wall; dried flowers in a Blue Nun bottle on a shelf behind the front door.

Jeannine Gramick has been a sister since 1960, but her work with gay Catholics did not start until 1971 when, as a graduate student at the University of Pennsylvania, she met a gay person at a "home liturgy." (Such experimental living-room masses were especially popular in Philadelphia, which was—and still is—among the most conservative archdioceses in the American church.)

"We started having home liturgies for gay people in his apartment," Gramick remembers. "The *Philadelphia Bulletin* ran an article about the masses, and Bob read it and wrote me a letter."

FOUNDING A SAFE HAVEN FOR THE GAY RELIGIOUS

Nugent was then a diocesan priest working in a parish in Levittown, north of Philadelphia. Gradually he became a regular celebrant of the home liturgies, began to counsel gay people, and read all he could find about homosexuality. When

Gramick was graduated from Penn, she was assigned to teach math at her order's college in Baltimore—safely out of reach of the Philadelphia church, which had begun to look askance at her work. Nugent remained in the City of Brotherly Love and later testified before the city council in favor of a gay-rights ordinance, in direct contradiction of the official archdiocesan position. (That bill and subsequent versions of it have been killed, largely due to church pressure; ironically, the archdiocese's official spokesman against gay rights was arrested early this year in New Orleans for making a homosexual advance to an undercover cop in a porno bookstore.)

In 1975, Nugent broke with the archdiocese and joined the Salvatorians, a religious order whose special interest is working for social justice. (Early in the seventies, the order's Task Force on Gay Rights wrote the first description of a possible Catholic ministry to gays.) The next year, he and Gramick moved to the Washington area to work on the staff of Quixote Center, a Catholic activist organization that lists gay rights among its many priorities for social change. Gramick and Nugent founded the New Ways Ministry last year.

"We both wanted to devote our full time to the gay issue," says Gramick. "We perceive a lot of hope and openness to what we're doing, in religious communities and in peace and justice groups. We did a workshop last summer in Los Angeles, and the Priests' Senate, the official organization of priests in the area, recommended that their members attend. Lots of them did, too."

New Ways also claims the sympathy, if not the outright support, of some Catholic bishops. "At least fifteen bishops could be called sympathetic to the need for a gay ministry," reports Gramick. "We received a financial contribution and a statement of support from one auxiliary bishop in New England, and a bishop in California told us that he supported our work, though he couldn't say so publicly." Neither bishop wanted his name mentioned by New Ways. Both Gramick and Nugent say that the priests and religious most interested in opening the church to gays are not gay themselves. "Gay clergy are far more homophobic than straight clergy," observes Gramick, "and it's the straight women religious who are speaking out on behalf of the gay women religious."

OBSTACLES ALONG THE WAY

New Ways Ministry has been in hot water with various ecclesiastical authorities almost since its inception. One of the reasons Jeannine Gramick and Bob Nugent seem able to persevere in their work is an uncanny ability to find silver linings in the most ominous clouds. Last December, for instance, a retreat that they were to conduct for Dignity [an organization for gay Catholics]/St. Louis almost did not take place. A crudely mimeographed, anonymous letter from "The Catholic Laymen's League of St. Michael the Archangel and St. Maria Goretti" was mailed to convents, parishes, and religious orders in St. Louis, denouncing the retreat as "Satanic." The circular made the archdiocese unhappy; after "consultation" with Cardinal Carberry of St. Louis, the Sisters of St. Joseph, who had offered a facility to New Ways for the weekend, withdrew their offer. The retreat did come off but in an abbreviated one-day version at the Catholic Worker Movement's local house of hospitality.

Despite the sabotage, Gramick and Nugent printed a list of the good effects of the St. Louis experience in the next issue of their newsletter:

> From the painful experience came . . . a dialogue between Dignity and the sisters who are interested in pursuing gay ministry; a dialogue between the sisters and Cardinal Carberry who acknowledges a need to do something more about ministry to gay Catholics; a reception for New Ways following the retreat that attracted more than a dozen area seminarians, brothers, sisters, and priests, including a provincial leader, a generalate staff member, and social justice coordinators . . . some positive publicity for Dignity/St. Louis . . . and a public acknowledgment of the Dignity retreat in an introduction of Jeannine and Bob to the worshipping community at College Church, St. Louis University, where

Bob celebrated Sunday liturgy in the church of the famous "St. Louis Jesuits."

Such experiences as the Dignity retreat were just skirmishes, however, compared to other trouble in store for Gramick and Nugent. Their major problems began when New Ways received a $38,000 grant from the National Institutes of Health for a two-year sociological study of "the coming-out processes and coping strategies" of gay women. The study is ground-breaking, according to a New Ways press release, because it "assumes that being gay is a valid expression of a person's life-style, involving more than the simple notion of sexual preference."

When the *Washington Star* (which seems to have been more than generous in its coverage of the gay Catholic issues) changed the word "gay" to "practicing homosexual" in a story about the study, the Washington archdiocese was quick to respond. An editorial in its official newspaper, the *Catholic Standard*, lambasted New Ways: "Homosexuals deserve justice, compassion, and every help in changing their way of life. But to try to legitimize homosexual activity is a disservice to homosexuals and a clear violation of the teachings of Christ and His Church."

A WEEKEND RETREAT CREATES NATIONAL CONTROVERSY

A month after the editorial appeared, another New Ways project engaged the archdiocese's interest, a project that would eventually involve the heads of Gramick's and Nugent's religious orders and the Vatican itself: a weekend retreat for gay nuns.

"There are groups of gay religious in touch with each other all over the country," explains Nugent. (Gramick has been forbidden by her religious superiors to discuss the retreat and will not say a word about it.) "Some of these groups have been meeting informally for recollection and prayer. A couple of the sisters involved asked us to coordinate and sponsor a weekend retreat. We weren't asked to take part in it, just to plan and schedule it."

New Ways sent out a mailing to women's communities throughout the country, announcing the retreat as "an historic event in the American Catholic Church." The letter also said, "While we are planning to give the event the widest possible publicity in the Catholic community and especially among communities of women religious, we are also sensitive to the need for respecting the privacy of the individual retreatants."

"Talking about 'the widest possible publicity' was a mistake," Nugent now admits. The letter leaked to the secular press. When a story about the proposed retreat appeared in the *Washington Post*, all hell broke loose.

Gramick's provincial superior, Sister Ruth Marie May, circulated a letter to everyone who had received the New Ways mailing. "Publicity which uses such terminology as 'gay women religious,'" she wrote, "I see not only as offensive and misleading, but ultimately detrimental to the present image and role of celibate women in a faith community. . . . While we do not deny that this orientation exists, we are nowhere near the time when we or the general public are equipped or integrated enough to handle the suspicion that this publicity evokes. . . . It would be well," she concluded, "to cancel the retreat."

The archdiocese of Washington was next to act. Its chancellor sent a terse statement to every Catholic bishop and religious provincial in the country, informing them that Gramick and Nugent "have not received permission or authorization to engage in any ministry within the archdiocese of Washington."

"Two years before," recalls Nugent, "we'd had members of the Priest's Senate of Washington and the priests' personnel board coming to our workshops. All of a sudden, without ever contacting us or asking what our work was about, the archdiocese decides we're unauthorized."

The chancellor's letter was followed by the removal of Nugent's faculties to say mass anywhere in Washington. Since New Ways was not an approved ministry, the logic ran, Nugent should not be allowed to promote that work by dispensing the sacraments as part of it. No other priest in Washington whose work lacked local church sanction has ever been thus disciplined, including such priests as Congressman Robert Drinan, the Jesuit Society of Jesus (S.J.) and Housing and Urban Development (HUD) Undersecretary Geno Baroni, who carry on unauthorized ministries as officials in the federal government.

Finally, the Vatican itself stepped into the controversy. "My order's superior general in Rome got the word from the Sacred Congregation of Religious that I was to cancel the retreat," says Nugent. But when the directive came down through channels to Nugent's immediate superior, Salvatorian provincial Myron Wagner, Wagner balked. Rome placed Wagner under "canonical obedience"—the little-used ecclesiastical equivalent of the army's "direct order"—to quash the retreat. Subsequently Robert Nugent was solemnly forbidden to organize the weekend. New Ways withdrew its sponsorship.

The retreat of gay sisters *did* take place—at an undisclosed location in the East, under Jeannine Gramick's sponsorship "as a person, not as a sister or part of New Ways." Nugent will not say how many sisters attended, but there were undoubtedly fewer than would have shown up had the fracas not occurred.

HOPE PREVAILS

What is next for New Ways? Gramick and Nugent spent the summer in England and the Netherlands, meeting with people engaged in gay ministries in those countries. They have scheduled two retreats for Catholic lesbians this fall. And they are planning a course called "Recycling Gay Catholics," for gay people who left the church before the Vatican Council and want to come back now. "It's not the same church they left," comments Nugent, despite his recent experiences.

One of New Ways Ministry's most ambitious and successful projects has been to organize the Catholic Coalition for Gay Civil Rights, whose members "urge all Catholics to support sound [gay] civil rights legislation on both federal and local levels." Over one thousand Catholic groups and individuals have endorsed the statement, including the National Coalition of American Nuns, the National Assembly of Religious Brothers, and many leading Catholic theologians and writers. The Catholic Coalition has not drawn the kind of attention New Ways' controversial retreats have, but it may be their most significant work—a gathering of America's leading Catholic thinkers that gives the lie to the spurious theology behind attacks on gay rights by church authorities in such cities as New York and Philadelphia.

GAY CLERGY—PROFILES IN COURAGE

I asked Jeannine Gramick if she could put me in touch with a gay nun who would be willing to talk about her experience. She promised to give my telephone number to the sister who had moderated the retreat for gay women religious. Two weeks later, "Sister Benedicta" called me.

Sister Benedicta (unlike most American nuns, she has not changed her religious name back to her family name) has a voice instantly recognizable to anyone who has ever attended Catholic elementary school. It is Sister's Voice—kind, sincere, and well-modulated, with an undercurrent of energy and a total absence of irony. I was surprised to find myself a bit flustered when that familiar voice started to describe her coming out.

"I'm not out publicly," said Sister Benedicta, "but I have come out to my reverend mother and some of the other sisters. Coming out was a long process for me. It took a couple of years. I was going to a priest for counseling. He told me that just because I felt attracted to other women didn't mean I was gay. Then a friend of mine, a brother, started to work with Dignity and I got involved too.

"My first reaction to dealing with my sexuality was one of struggling to become more knowledgeable about myself. I wanted to run. I wouldn't let anyone else know. But gradually I came to accept it.

"I've done a little experimentation and have come to the conclusion that I must live celibate—that is, without genital sex. I know that there are others in religious life who choose a different way. There are people for whom celibacy means don't get involved with one person. There are others for whom sex is an expression of friendship and deep sharing.

"Right now, I have no tension with my vocation. Everything I've done, my reverend mother knows about. Of course, I wouldn't want it to get back to Rome."

Sister Benedicta entered religious life in 1950, a year after she graduated from high school. She describes herself as coming "from a very conservative family background." Her order, a small missionary community, has been "very accepting of me; they don't seem frightened by my being gay."

She refuses to discuss the retreat she moderated. "I think if anything else comes out about it, we'll have the bloodhounds on us," she says. "Right now, the important thing to do is help people. Every major superior is confronted with the issue. We just have to be careful about getting the issue out in the open without crucifying individuals.

"Some people challenge me," says Sister Benedicta. "They say, 'If you really believe in what you're saying, then stand up and shout about it.' But that's really not an option for me."

BUILDING A RELATIONSHIP BETWEEN SEXUALITY AND RELIGION

Sister Benedicta is one of hundreds of gay religious who, without shouting, are exploring the meaning of their sexual orientation in the life they have chosen to lead. So far there is one national newsletter in which gay sisters, brothers, and priests can share the fruits of that exploration. It is a measure of the loneliness and risk involved in that effort that every person I asked about the newsletter urged me not to publish its name, the city where it is edited, or the identities of its editors (who only use their first names, in any case).

I will not break that confidence. But I will mention the newsletter's subtitle: "A dialogue on the relationship between personal sexuality and ministry for the purpose of building community among gay clergy and religious." The publication is written by gay religious from around the country, and while the writing lacks polish, it bears moving testimony to a process of reflection that, much more than a specific function like "teaching" or "saying mass," defines what Catholic religious life is all about. The following lines from a priest in the Midwest capture some of the pain and hopefulness of that process:

> When I entered religious life, I was certain that religion was my only bid for a life of human dignity and morality. Homosexuality was a curse to be escaped. Later on, I felt it was a cross, gratuitously given, to be nobly born [sic]. Then I began to discover that my sexuality was the source of most of my personality traits that I valued and found effective in ministry. Now it is clear to me that my gayness is a key for growth and health and relationship.

> A friend of mine once quipped ... that he was a practicing homosexual and intended to continue practicing until he was good at it. I feel the need, with great insistence, to integrate and perfect my gayness, to practice until I am good at it. What that means really in the context of celibate life, I do not yet know. ... I do know for certain that I must find a way of replacing the cycle of repression and depression that I have inflicted on myself as a way of "reconciling" my sexuality and my vows with some as yet undiscovered pattern of expression and celebration.

In Good Times and in Bad: The Vermont Civil Union Law Provides Equal Rights for Same-Sex Couples

PAULA ETTELBRICK

Paula Ettelbrick is the Family Policy Director in the National Gay and Lesbian Task Force (NGLTF) Policy Institute. In the following selection, she presents an overview of Vermont's Civil Union Law, which was passed in April 2000. This law provides same-sex couples with the same rights, privileges, and responsibilities as heterosexual married couples, including dependent health insurance coverage, hospital visitation, emergency care decisions, estate inheritance, and Social Security survivor benefits.

While opponents argue that this law threatens the institution of marriage and will contribute to the moral decay of our country, Ettelbrick points out that these same "alarms were sounded in your great-great-grandmother's day, as these were the responses to the mid–nineteenth century wave of Married Women's Property Acts, passed both in the United States and Britain. . . . Most would agree that women's independence from their husbands hardly resulted in the demise of civilization."

This law will "abolish family in the old sense," "virtually destroy the moral and social efficacy of the marriage institution," and is "contrary . . . to the law of God." Sound familiar? We hear this anytime someone raises the issue of whether lesbian and gay couples should be able to enter into civil marriage. But these "destruction-of-the-family" alarms were also sounded in your great-great-grandmother's day, as these were the responses to the mid-19th Century wave of Married Women's Property Acts, passed both in the United States and Britain. Those laws granted married women independent legal and economic status, allowing them to own property in their own right—a right that was lost only upon marriage. Most would agree that women's independence from their husbands hardly resulted in the demise of civilization. Yet, anytime one tinkers with the basic principles of marriage (something that happens every other generation or so), someone is out there decrying the fall of civilization.

In five short, frenzied months, Vermont has leapt ahead of the national pack by ushering in yet another change to the official rules of marriage and family structure as defined by state laws across the country. In April the Vermont legislature, working under the mandate of the state supreme court, adopted a Civil Union Law. The new law, effective July 1, 2000, allows lesbian and gay couples to "certify" their relationships with the county clerks' offices in Vermont. Once certified, they will receive the exact same benefits, rights and privileges, and will be beholden to the same responsibilities and burdens, as any heterosexual married couple. If history is any guide, the world will not fall apart on July 2 or anytime thereafter when gay couples are able for the first time in history to access all of the legal benefits of marriage in the single state of Vermont.

The developments in Vermont started when two lesbian couples and a gay male couple challenged the Vermont state law that limits marriage to only a man and a woman. As citizens and taxpayers, they claimed they should have the same "common benefits" of marriage that the state provides automatically to married couples. The court agreed that the state constitution requires that same-sex couples should receive the same benefits of marriage, and threw the whole matter onto the citizen legislature of Vermont to decide how to accomplish this mandate. Significantly, the court and the legislature stopped short of calling the relationship between two women or two men a "marriage." Fearful, undoubtedly, of infringing the trademark that heterosexuals have implicitly claimed over the name "marriage," the legislature created an entirely new structure under the civil union law. Couples are "certified," not married. Should they break-up, they seek "dissolution" through the courts, not divorce. The name by which one refers to a civil union partner is still up for grabs, but undoubtedly many will use the legal term of art, "spouse." From a legal perspective, marriage and civil unions extend the same benefits.

Lesbian and gay couples will go to the nearest county clerk to certify their relationships under the new law for the same reason that straight couples get married—for love. Like anyone else, most gay and lesbian couples want their love to be publicly acknowledged to the community family and friends that they will call upon for support in tough times. They want to be a part of this social compact of marriage.

Protecting Families as Well as Rights

They will also formalize their relationships as civil unions in order to protect their families. Having stood on the margins of family for so long, gay and lesbian couples are more attuned than most to the importance of formal family recognition to gaining access to the thousands of benefits and protections extended by law and custom in our society. Employees may get health care coverage for their spouses and children. Doctors will consult with spouses and allow them to make life and death decisions for an ill partner, over any other family member's dissent. The state may not require spouses to testify against each other in a court of law. Federal law requires employers to allow employees to take medical or family leave to care for an ill spouse or welcome a new baby without fear of losing their job. A spouse who is a citizen of another country may immigrate to the United States in order to keep the family together. A surviving spouse is entitled to his partner's social security

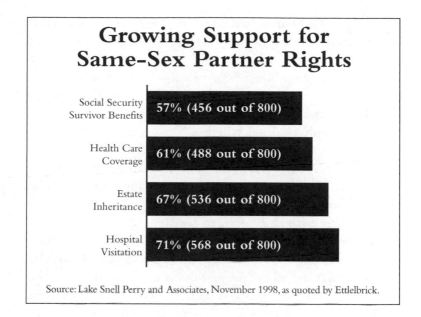

Growing Support for Same-Sex Partner Rights

Social Security Survivor Benefits	57% (456 out of 800)
Health Care Coverage	61% (488 out of 800)
Estate Inheritance	67% (536 out of 800)
Hospital Visitation	71% (568 out of 800)

Source: Lake Snell Perry and Associates, November 1998, as quoted by Ettlelbrick.

benefits, has advantages under inheritance tax laws, and is the automatic administrator of the estate entitled to make all decisions about the property and belongings of the deceased.

These privileges emanate from our social desire to support and secure family structures. We believe deeply that all of us live much more productive, healthy lives when we are part of a social unit called family. In fact, research shows greater levels of mental and physical health among those who share companionship through marriage. We believe that those who commit their lives to one another have the obligation to care for each other, and we help them do so through laws and policies directed at supporting family. Because the access point to this public support is usually marriage, gay and lesbian couples have been uniquely disqualified from even the most basic acknowledgement of our relationships.

Particularly in tough times, our families need these protections to cope and care for one another just like anyone else. The story of Karen Thompson and Sharon Kowalski, a lesbian couple who lived together in St. Cloud, MN is illustrative. In 1983, Karen received a call late one November afternoon telling her that Sharon had been in a terrible car accident. Karen rushed to the hospital, arriving well before any of Sharon's other family members, who lived much further away. She asked the nurse about Sharon's condition. The nurse refused any information because Karen was not a family member. She continued to track down doctors and other administrators to simply find out whether Sharon was dead or alive. No one would give her even that level of basic information. Hours passed. It was not until Sharon's parents arrived that Karen learned that her loved one was still alive, but would be severely disabled due to a near fatal close-head injury. As Sharon started the slow path to recovery, her parents got a court order excluding Karen from visiting or in any way continuing contact with her partner since they had no legal relationship. After a costly eight year court battle, Karen won the right to maintain her relationship with Sharon and they were reunited. Now, 10 years later, Karen provides daily care to Sharon who cannot walk, speak, eat or dress on her own, or carry on many of life's functions. Karen has done all of this without any of the social or legal benefits that are there to assist other families in coping with such a tragedy.

The civil union law for same-sex couples is not about destroying heterosexual marriage. It is not about forcing religions to perform gay unions. In fact, many religious denominations are well ahead of political bodies in voluntarily performing marriage ceremonies for lesbian and gay couples. Instead, the Vermont law addresses the government's obligation to treat its citizens equally. It is a state response to the diversity that we usually trumpet except in cases of family and marriage, where one size is supposed to fit all. It is part of our nation's greater discussion—and consternation—about how to address the needs of changing family structures.

ALL CITIZENS ARE ENTITLED TO EQUAL TREATMENT UNDER THE LAW

Rather, the sole purpose of the Vermont civil union law is to treat gay and lesbian people as equal citizens by extending the same benefits to them that are given to heterosexual married couples. It is a goal that the majority of Americans support. A November 1998 poll by Lake Snell Perry and Associates found that the majority of people support the following benefits for gay couples: hospital visitation rights (71%), inheritance rights to a partner's property (67%), Social Security spousal benefits (57%) and domestic partner health care coverage (61%). While it is true that most Americans do not support "marriage" for lesbian and gay couples, a 1997 poll showed that 56% of Washington State voters opposed laws that affirmatively "withhold legal status to same-gender marriages performed in another state." A majority of both Democratic voters (58%) as well as Republican voters (52%) opposed these exclusionary measures. On issues of basic equality, 83% of Americans support equal rights to employment, according to a 1999 Gallup Poll, and 75% support equal housing rights for lesbians and gay men, as found in a 1998 Princeton Survey Research Associates poll.

Recognition of same-sex unions is likely to move beyond Vermont for three reasons. First, the tide is shifting against the groundless vitriol of the anti-gay right. By zeroing in on Americans' discomfort with sexuality and focussing obsessively on sex acts, the anti-gay right has painted a gruesome picture of lesbians and gay men as lustful, leering beasts who want nothing other than to recruit your children to Sodom and Gomorrah. These are lies. Common sense tells us that these are lies. Fear mongering is a classic tactic for justifying unjustifiable behavior toward another human being. The Japanese internment during World War II was accomplished through exploiting people's fear of a wartime enemy and projecting it on to Japanese-American citizens an ocean away. The use of overly sexualized images to monger such fear is a common tactic for scaring people into rejecting the basic humanity of certain people and adopting repressive laws that keep these groups suppressed. Black men are commonly sexualized as a way of stoking fear and in the years preceding the Holocaust the Nazis demonized the Jews as child predators.

Second, families have changed. It always changes in response to political, cultural and economic forces. Marriage is no longer the only organizing principle for families. The Census Bureau recognized this fact in 1990 when it started counting unmarried partners. City agencies try to accommodate this fact. Thousands of employers who provide domestic partnership benefits for unmarried partners know this. The Supreme Court recognized this by taking the rare family law case, this one considering whether grandparents should have legal rights of visitation over a parent's objection. France, Australia, Denmark, Norway, Hungary and a growing number of other nations have constructed new family models that have moved beyond heterosexual marriage. Moderate and conservative scholars have recognized the full force of cultural changes that require a fresh look at how we structure and support families. Vermont's full support for same-sex unions may be among the most dramatic changes in this country, but it will surely not be the last.

Third, lesbians and gay men are indisputably a part of the diversity of this nation. What has made marriage such a durable institution is not its emphasis on conformity, but rather its ability to flex and change to accommodate the purposes for which it exists. In the 21st Century, those goals are different from what they were 100 or 500 years ago. Marriage no longer exists for the purpose of forging great dynasties or securing one's lineage or keeping blood lines "clean." Today, people marry the person they love for companionship and support. Some marry because they know that raising children and providing them with a secure environment is best accomplished by a team. These purposes are not contingent on sexual orientation or gender. They are universal. To serve these goals, government's singular role should be to help all who make a commitment along these lines to flourish. That includes lesbian and gay couples.

CHAPTER 4

THE GAY COUNTER-CULTURE: CONFRONTING CONSERVATISM IN THE MOVEMENT

AMERICAN
SOCIAL
MOVEMENTS

The Lesbian Butch-Fem Relationship Is Not a Heterosexual Mock-Up

JOAN NESTLE

Joan Nestle is cofounder of the Lesbian Herstory Archives and the
Lesbian Herstory Educational Foundation. In the following selection
she laments the continual misunderstanding of the butch-fem relationship: "In the past, the butch has been labeled too simplistically
the masculine partner and the fem her feminine counterpart. This
labeling forgets two women who have developed their styles for specific erotic, emotional, and social reasons."

A self-proclaimed fem, Nestle uses her own experiences as well
as her research into the past as a means to explore the true nature of
the butch-fem relationship and the resistance to it from both outside and inside the gay rights movement.

For many years now, I have been trying to figure out how
to explain the special nature of butch-fem relationships to
feminists and lesbian feminists who consider butch-fem a re-
production of heterosexual models, and therefore dismiss both
lesbian communities of the past and of the present that assert
this style. Before I continue, my editor wants me to define the
term butch-fem, and I am overwhelmed at the complexity of
the task. Living a butch-fem life was not an intellectual exercise; it was not a set of theories. Deep in my gut I know what
being a fem has meant to me, but it is very hard to articulate
this identity in a way that does justice to its fullest nature and

Joan Nestle, "The Fem Question," *Pleasure and Danger: Exploring Female Sexuality*, edited
by Carole S. Vance. London: Pandora Press, 1992. Copyright © 1984 by Joan Nestle. Reproduced by permission.

yet answers the questions of a curious reader. In the most basic terms, butch-fem means a way of looking, loving, and living that can be expressed by individuals, couples or a community. In the past, the butch has been labeled too simplistically the masculine partner and the fem her feminine counterpart. This labeling forgets two women who have developed their styles for specific erotic, emotional, and social reasons. Butch-fem relationships, as I experienced them, were complex erotic and social statements, not phony heterosexual replicas. They were filled with a deeply lesbian language of stance, dress, gesture, love, courage, and autonomy. In the 1950s particularly, butch-fem couples were the front-line warriors against sexual bigotry. Because they were so visibly obvious, they suffered the brunt of street violence. The irony of social change has made a radical, sexual, political statement of the 1950s appear today as a reactionary, non-feminist experience. My own roots lie deep in the earth of this lesbian custom and what follows is one lesbian's understanding of her own experience.

I am a fem and have been for over twenty-five years. I know the reaction this statement gets now: many lesbians dismiss me as a victim, a woman who could do nothing else because she didn't know any better, but the truth of my life tells a different story. We fems helped hold our lesbian world together in an unsafe time. We poured out more love and wetness on our barstools and in our homes than women were supposed to have. I have no theories to explain how the love came, why the crushes on the lean dark women exploded in my guts, made me so shy that all I could do was look so hard that they had to move away. But I wasn't a piece of fluff and neither were the other fems I knew. We knew what we wanted and that was no mean feat for young women of the 1950s, a time when the need for conformity, marriage and babies was being trumpeted at us by the government's policy makers. Oh, we had our styles—our outfits, our perfumes, our performances—and we could lose ourselves under the chins of our dancing partners who held us close enough to make the world safe; but we walked the night streets to get to our bars, and we came out bleary-eyed into the deserted early morning, facing a long week of dreary passing at the office or the beauty parlor or the telephone company. I always knew our lives were a bewildering combination of romance and realism. I could tell you stories . . .

about the twenty-year-old fem who carried her favorite dildo in a pink satin purse to the bar every Saturday night so her partner for the evening would understand exactly what she wanted . . .

or how at seventeen I hung out at Pam Pam's on Sixth Avenue and Eighth Street in Greenwich Village with all the other fems who were too young to get into the bars and too inexperienced to know how to forge an ID. We used this bare, tired coffee shop as a training ground, a meeting place to plan the night's forays. Not just fems—young butches were there too, from all the boroughs, taking time to comb their hair just the right way in the mirror beside the doorway . . .

or how I finally entered my world, a bar on Abingdon Square, where I learned that women had been finding each other for years, and how as young fems we took on the Vice Squad, the plainclothes police women, the bathroom line with its allotted amount of toilet paper, the Johns trying to hustle a woman for the night and the staring straights who saw us as entertaining freaks. My passion had taken me home and not all the hating voices of the McCarthy 1950s could keep me away from my community.

A History of Empowerment and Harsh Judgments

Every time I speak at a lesbian-feminist gathering, I introduce myself as a fem who came out in the 1950s. I do this, because it is the truth and therefore allows me to pay historical homage to my lesbian time and place, to the women who have slipped away, yet whose voices I still hear and whose V-necked sweaters and shiny loafers I still see. I do it to call up the women I would see shopping with their lovers in the Lower East Side supermarkets, the fem partners of the butch women who worked as waiters in the Club 82. I remember how unflinchingly the fem absorbed the stares of the other customers as she gently held onto the arm of her partner. Butches were known by their appearances, fems by their choices. I do it in the name of the wives of passing women [lesbians who look like men to the straight world] whose faces look up at me from old newspaper clippings, the women whom reporters described as the deceived ones and yet whose histories suggest much more complicated choices. And if fems seemed to be "wives" of passing women, the feminine protectors of the couple's propriety, it was so easy to lose curiosity about what made them sexual heretics, because they looked like women. Thus fems became the victims of a double dismissal: in the past they did not appear culturally different enough from heterosexual women to be seen as breaking gender taboos and today they do not appear feminist enough, even in their historical context, to merit attention or respect for being groundbreaking women.

If we are to piece together a profound feminist and lesbian history, we must begin asking questions about the lives of these women that we have not asked before, and to do this we will have to elevate curiosity to a much more exalted position than concepts of politically correct sexuality would ever allow us to do. Politically correct sexuality is a paradoxical concept. One of the most deeply held opinions in feminism is that women should be autonomous and self-directed in defining their sexual desire, yet when a woman says, "This is my desire," feminists rush in to say, "No, no, it is the prick in your head; women should not desire that act." But we do not yet know enough at all about what women—any women—desire. The real problem here is that we stopped asking questions so early in the lesbian and feminist movement, that we rushed to erect what appeared to be answers into the formidable and rigid edifice that it is now. Our contemporary lack of curiosity also affects our view of the past. We don't ask butch-fem women who they are; we tell them. We don't explore the social life of working-class lesbian bars in the 1940s and 1950s; we simply assert that all those women were victims. Our supposed answers closed our ears and stopped our analysis. Questions and answers about lesbian lives that deviate from the feminist model of the 1970s strike like a shock wave against the movement's foundation, yet this new wave of questioning is an authentic one, coming from women who have helped create the feminist and lesbian movement that they are now challenging into the new growth. If we close down exploration, we will be forcing some women once again to live their sexual lives in a land of shame and guilt; only this time they will be haunted by the realization that it was not the patriarchal code they have failed, but the creed of their own sisters who said they came in love. Curiosity builds bridges between women and between the present and the past; judgment builds the power of some over others. Curiosity is not trivial; it is the respect one life pays to another. It is a largeness of mind and heart that refuses to be bounded by decorum or by desperation. It is hardest to keep alive in the times it is most needed, the times of hatred, of instability, of attack. Surely these are such times.

A STYLE OF RESISTANCE VERSUS REPLICATION

When I stand before a new generation of lesbians and use this word "fem," I sometimes feel very old, like a relic from a long-buried past that has burst through the earth, shaken the dust off its mouth and started to speak. The first reaction is usually shock and then laughter and then confusion, when my audience must confront their stereotyped understanding of this word and yet face the fact that I am a powerful woman who has done some good in this brave new world of lesbian feminism. But the audience is not the only one who is going through waves of reactions. I too wonder how will I be perceived through these layers of history. A 1980s lesbian activist who defines herself as a fem poses the problem of our plight as an oppressed people in a most vivid way.

Colonization and the battle against it always poses a contradiction between appearances and deeper survivals. There is a need to reflect the colonizer's image back at him yet at the same time to keep alive what is a deep part of one's culture, even if it can be misunderstood by the oppressor, who omnipotently thinks he knows what he is seeing. Butch-fem carries all this cultural warfare with it. It appears to incorporate elements of the heterosexual culture in power; it is disowned by some who want to make a statement against the pervasiveness of this power, yet it is a valid style, matured in years of struggle and harboring some of our bravest women. The colonizer's power enforces not only a daily cultural devaluing but also sets up a memory trap, forcing us to devalue what was resistance in the past in a desperate battle to be different from what they say we are.

Both butches and fems have a history of ingenuity in the creation of personal style, but since the elements of this style—the clothing, the stance—come from the heterosexually defined culture, it is easy to confuse an innovative or resisting style with a mere replica of the prevailing custom. But a butch lesbian wearing men's clothes in the 1950s was not a man wearing men's clothes; she was a woman who created an original style to signal to other women what she was capable of doing—taking erotic responsibility. In the feminist decades, the fem is the lesbian who poses this problem of misinterpreted choice in the deepest way. If we dress to please ourselves and the other women to whom we want to announce our desire, we are called traitors by many of our own community, because we seem to be wearing the clothes of the enemy. Make-up, high heels, skirts, revealing clothes, even certain ways of holding the body are read as capitulation to patriarchal control of women's bodies. An accurate critique, if a woman feels uncomfortable or forced to present herself this way, but this is not what I am doing when I feel sexually powerful and want to share it with other women. Fems are women who have made choices, but we need to be able to read between the cultural lines to appreciate their strength. Lesbians should be mistresses of discrepancies, knowing that resistance lies in the change of context.

The message to fems throughout the 1970s was that we were the Uncle Toms of the movement. If I wore the acceptable movement clothes of sturdy shoes, dungarees, work shirt and back pack, then I was to be trusted, but that is not always how I feel strongest. If I wear these clothes, because I am afraid of the judgment of my own people, then I am a different kind of traitor, this time to my own fem sense of personal style, since this style represents what I have chosen to do with my womanness. I cannot hide it or exchange it without losing my passion or my strength. The saddest irony of all behind this misjudgment of fems is that for many of us it has been a life-long journey to take pleasure in our bodies. Butch lovers, reassuring and kind, passionate and taking, were for many of us a bridge back to acceptance of what the society around us told us to scorn: big-hipped, wide-assed women's bodies. My idiosyncratic sexual history leads me to express my feminist victories in my own way; other women, straight or gay, carry these victories of personal style within, hesistant to publicly display them, because they fear the judgment of the women's community. Our understanding of resistance is thus deeply diminished.

In the 1970s and 1980s, the fem is also charged with the crime of passing, of trying to disassociate herself from the androgynous lesbian. In the earlier decades, many fems used their appearance to secure jobs that would allow their butch lovers to dress and live the way they both wanted her to. Her fem appearance allowed her to pass over into enemy lines to make economic survival possible. But when butches and fems of this style went out together, no one could accuse the fem of passing. In fact, the more extremely fem she was, the more obvious was their lesbianism and the more street danger they faced. Now lesbian style occurs in the context of a more and more androgynous appearing society, and fem dress becomes even more problematic. A fem is often seen as a lesbian acting like a straight woman who is not a feminist—a terrible misreading of self-presentation which turns a language of liberated desire into the silence of collaboration. An erotic conversation between two women is completely unheard, not by men this time but by other women, many in the name of lesbian-feminism.

When one carries the fem identity into the arena of political activism, the layers of confusion grow. In the Spring of 1982, Deborah, my lover, and I did the Lesbian Herstory Archives slide show at the Stony Brook campus of the State University of New York (SUNY). We were speaking to fifty women health workers, four of whom identified themselves as lesbians. I wore a long lavender dress that made my body feel good and high, black boots that made me feel powerful. Deb was dressed in pants, shirt, vest and leather jacket. I led a two-hour discussion working with the women's honest expressions of homophobia, their fears of seeing their own bodies sexually, and the different forms of tyranny they faced as women. Finally one of the straight women said how much easier it was to talk to me rather than to Deb, who was sitting at the side of the room. "I look more like you," she said pointing to me. She too was wearing a long dress and boots. Here my appearance, which was really an erotic conversation between Deb and myself, was transformed into a boundary line between us. I walked over to Deb, put my arm around her and drew her head into my breasts. "Yes," I said, "but it is the two of us together that make everything perfectly clear." Then I returned to the center of the room and lied. "I wore this dress so you would listen to me but our real freedom is the day when I can wear a three-piece suit and tie and you will still hear my words." I found myself faced with the paradox of having to fight for one freedom at the price of another. The audience felt more comfortable with me because I could pass, yet their misunderstanding of my femness was betraying its deepest meaning.

Because I am on the defensive many times in raising these issues, it is tempting to gloss over the difficulties that did exist in the past and do now. Being a fem was never a simple experience, not in the old lesbian bars of the 1950s and not now. Fems were deeply cherished and yet devalued as well. There were always fem put-down jokes going around the bar, while at the same time tremendous energy and caring was spent courting the fem women. We were not always trusted and often seen as the more flighty members of the lesbian world, a contradiction to our actual lives where we all knew fems who had stood by their butch lovers through years of struggle. We were mysterious and practical, made homes and broke them up, were glamorous and boring all at the same time. Butches and fems had an internal dialogue to work out, but when the police invaded our bars, when we were threatened with physical violence, when taunts and jeers followed us down the streets, this more subtle discussion was transformed into a monolithic front where both butch and fem struggled fiercely to protect each other against the attackers. Feminists need to know much more about how fems perceived themselves and how they were seen by those who loved them. Certainly the erotic clarity that was for me and many other fems at the heart of our style has never been clearly understood by sexologists or by feminists.

WE CANNOT BE STRIPPED OF OUR POWER

Since the butch–fem tradition is one of the oldest in lesbian culture, it came under investigation along with everything else when the sexologists began their study of sexual deviance. The feminine invert, as fems were called then, was viewed as the imperfect deviant. The sexology literatures from 1909 stated that the "pure female invert feels like a man." A few years later, the fem is described as an "effeminate tribadist [lesbian]." In the 1950s, our pathology was explained this way:

> The feminine type of Lesbian is one who seeks mother love, who enjoys being a recipient of much attention and affection. She is often preoccupied with personal beauty and is somewhat narcissistic. . . . She is the clinging vine type who is often thought and spoken of by her elders as a little fool without any realization of the warped sexuality which is prompting her actions.

And then the doctor adds the final blow: "She is more apt to be bisexual and also apt to respond favorably to treatment." Here the fem lesbian is stripped of all power, made into a foolish woman who can easily be beckoned over into the right camp. Historically, we have been left disinherited, seen neither as true inverts nor as grown women.

An example from early twentieth-century lesbian literature also shows the complexity of the fem tradition. In *The Well of Loneliness*, published in 1928, two major fem characters embody some of the mythic characteristics of fems. One is an unhappy wife who seduces Stephen Gordon, the butch heroine, but then betrays her, choosing the security of a safe life. The other is Beth, the lover Stephen turns over to a future husband at the end of the novel so she may have a chance at a "normal" life, thus enabling the author to make a plea for greater understanding of the deviant's plight. The reality of the author's life, however, gives a different portrait of a fem woman. Lady Una Troubridge, the partner of Radclyffe Hall, who saw herself as Hall's wife, was a major force in getting *The Well of Loneliness* published, even though she knew it would open their lives to turmoil and worse:

> She [Radclyffe Hall] came to me, telling me that in her view the time was ripe, and that although the publication of such a book might mean the shipwreck of her whole career, she was fully prepared to make any sacrifice except— the sacrifice of my peace of mind.

> She pointed out that in view of our union and of all the years that we had shared a home, what affected her must also affect me and that I would be included in any condemnation. Therefore she placed the decision in my hands and would write or refrain as I should decide. I am glad to remember that my reply was made without so much as an instant's hesitation: I told her to write what was in her heart, that so far as any effect upon myself was concerned, I was sick to death of ambiguities, and only wished to be known for what I was and to dwell with her in the palace of truth.

Why Radclyffe Hall with this steadfast fem woman by her side could not portray the same type of woman in her lesbian novel is a topic that needs further exploration. Troubridge's cry, "I am sick of ambiguities," could become a fem's motto.

What this very brief examination of examples from sexology and literature points out, I hope, is how much more we need to know, to question, to explore. Fems have been seen as a problem through the decades both by those who never pretended to be our friends and now by those who say they are our comrades. The outcry over the inclusion of a discussion of butch-fem relationships in the Barnard [College] sexuality conference [in 1982] was a shock to me; I had waited for over ten years for this part of my life to be taken seriously by a feminist gathering. I marched, demonstrated, conferenced, leafleted, CRed [consciousness-raised] my way through the 1970s, carrying this past and the women who had lived it deep within me, believing that when we had some safe territory, we could begin to explore what our lives had really meant. Yet even raising the issue, even entertaining the possibility that we were not complete victims but had some sense of what we were doing, was enough to encourage a call for silence by feminists who feared our voices. Those of us who want to begin talking again are not the reactionary backlash against feminism, as some would call us. We are an outgrowth of the best of feminism in a new time, trying to ask questions about taboo territories, trying to understand how women in the past and now have had the strength and the courage to express desire and resistance. We ask these questions in the service of the belief that women's lives are our deepest text, even the life of a fem.

The Challenges Facing the Bisexual Liberation Movement

REBECCA SHUSTER

Rebecca Shuster explores the oppression of bisexuals, which continues not only in the heterosexual community but in the gay community as well. As a bisexual, Shuster notes that despite some gains—such as legal recognition and the growth of support networks nationwide—several challenges remain to abolishing discrimination based on sexual identity and gender.

Shuster is a psychotherapist, teacher, and author of *Sexuality as a Continuum: The Bisexual Identity*.

As bisexual people, we are united in the goal and dream of ending the oppression of bisexuals, and a wider vision of eradicating all oppression. As we move toward the establishment of an organized constituency, taking this early opportunity to review the current state of bisexual liberation and the strong and the weak points in our efforts to date can assist us to formulate the most effective strategies for the next period. We can then develop and act on a liberation program that will, piece by piece, dismantle institutionalized oppression, individual participation in oppression, and the effects of internalized oppression on our lives and our organizations.

We have done well. Individually and collectively, we have made great strides. Bisexual organizations have germinated nationally and internationally, initiating support groups, newsletters, dances, lesbian and gay pride march contingents, and conferences. Those who have folded newsletters, convened the first daring support groups, told their stories in the lesbian, gay, and mainstream press, etc., deserve praise and thanks. These political, social, and textual meeting places provided forums to heal, to think, to forge vital redefinitions of societal concepts of closeness and sexual identity, and to take action. There we have learned about the mechanics of bisexual and lesbian and gay oppression and the resulting injury of all people: bisexuals, lesbians and gay men, and heterosexuals.

Within and outside our organizations, bisexuals play a pivotal role toward flexibility of sexual choice and identity. Many bisexuals understand and courageously act on the knowledge that identity is useful as a tool for personal and world evolution but not as a limitation on any human being. We are increasingly able to set up the broad strokes and passing moments of our lives without the imposition of those constructs. We speak out against sexual harassment in our workplaces, where we are often assumed to be heterosexual. We volunteer in AIDS hospices, often assumed to be lesbians and gay men.

In addition, many bisexuals understand and act on the importance of building a wide range of close relationships, sexual or not, with both women and men. Many bisexuals aim to bar societal assumptions about gender from bearing on our love, and our lives are outstanding models for weaving networks of tender, committed relationships.

These wise, creative, bold decisions to seek to define ourselves and sculpt closeness free of the prescribed restrictions on women, men, affection, and sexuality have given us a particular willingness to hold out a vision of human potential, do independent thinking, respect others with diverse life choices, and be liberation leaders for many social change movements.

We can be proud and pleased.

REMAINING CHALLENGES

The mainstream media sometimes lists bisexuals among populations battling AIDS, and some lesbian and gay organizations have added the word "bisexual" to their names. But we cannot mistake the visibility we have gained for genuine advances in our liberation any more than saying civil rights laws which guarantee the rights of people of color can be celebrated as an end to racism. Misconceptions about and intolerance toward bisexuals remain rampant in heterosexual, lesbian, and gay cultures. Bisexuals continue to be considered profiteers of heterosexual privilege, indecisive, untrustworthy, exotic, incapable of committed relationships, promiscuous, and responsible for the spread of AIDS. Bisexuals face vicious, systematic mistreatment, enforced with violence and threats of violence. That oppression, in all its glaring and hidden forms, is largely internalized, leaving bisexuals with a distorted self-image that prevents us from flourishing and hinders leadership development.

To eradicate bisexuals' internalized oppression, we must begin to identify the forms it can take:

• *Political and personal homelessness:* Repeated rejection in the lesbian, gay, and heterosexual communities leaves bisexuals feeling as though we are not welcome anywhere and do not fit anywhere. As a result, we are often suspicious, defensively "covering all our bases" as if attack can come from any corner at any time, and skeptically testing out those we meet to somehow determine if they can be trusted.

• *Marginalization:* Bisexuals often internalize the accusation that we are odd or strange and accept a place outside of all that is established, "mainstream," or usual. This view leads us to political errors, confusing potential allies for "the enemy."

• *Hiding (in the closet):* Bisexuals often conceal who we are— our assets as well as our difficulties—in the hopes of protecting ourselves from intolerance. Thus, we often act on pretense, losing the ability to detect the actual degree of safety in each specific situation.

• *Refusal to choose:* Because we long to reach our full potentials, we often feel that deciding to commit ourselves to one person, one career, etc. is inherently limiting or suffocating. Profound vows to maintain open options often underlie our identities as bisexuals, sometimes rooted in past experiences in which we were forced to make unnecessary and emotionally costly choices. Those vows can leave us unwilling to close any door, even to do what is right. We may be overdiversified and spread thin, attempting to substitute "equal opportunity" and a lack of affiliation for genuinely ending oppression.

• *Gender confusion:* Bisexuals sometimes do not feel or define themselves as wholly male or female. In our earnest desire to dissolve gender roles, we may pretend to achieve androgyny, as if women's and men's liberation can be accomplished without the arduous and powerful work of unraveling the effects of this oppression and realizing liberation for all women and men.

• *Superiority:* Because we have been forced to defend ourselves again and again, bisexuals often justify our difficulties not only as strengths, but as preferred lifestyle. Bisexuality is not better than any other sexual identity, and to act as if this were the case keeps us gravely divided from lesbians, gay men, and heterosexuals.

In particular, bisexuals often defend our sexual practices as superior to those of heterosexuals, lesbians, and gay men. While bisexuals are often leaders toward sexual freedom, selecting partners of both genders is not by itself equivalent to liberation. All young people raised in this culture absorb debilitating mythology about sexuality, and far more frequently than we have yet acknowledged or documented, are the victims of sexual abuse. These experiences impede the ability to intelligently choose sexual partners and activities, regardless of sexual identity. Since bisexuals are not raised differently from the rest of the culture, we therefore act on the same kinds of sexual compulsion, inhibition, and confusion as our heterosexual, lesbian, and gay friends.

The task before us is to design a strategy which will most rapidly eliminate any oppression and internalized oppression that hinders bisexuals' lives. There is much work to be done.

Where bisexuals have begun to become visible and build organizations, a division between bisexuals and lesbians and gay men has often been created that is a key barrier to our success. As a starting point, bisexuals must understand that those who are labeled or identify as bisexual are subject to the identical mistreatment as lesbians and gay men to the degree to which we challenge gender-based stereotypes. If we review the content of the oppression and internalized oppression of bisexuals listed above, it becomes clear that our experience is simply a form of lesbian and gay oppression, not a separate oppression. When a lesbian, gay man, or bisexual is perpetuating a bisexual's oppression, she or he is acting out of internalized oppression. When a heterosexual plays that role, she or he is acting as an agent of the oppression.

Because the oppression of bisexuals is lesbian and gay oppression, bisexuals are, in part, a constituency *within* lesbian and gay liberation. To define bisexuals' oppression as distinct from lesbian and gay oppression is divisive and slows the fulfillment of our goals. Like sections of the working class, we cannot permit ourselves to be pitted against one another but instead must unite against our common oppression.

At the same time, bisexuals are a constituency within heterosexuality. When we are assumed to be heterosexual and participate in heterosexual relationships, activities, and institutions, we reap the benefits and sustain the limitations of heterosexuality. To deny this part of our lives is vain and as destructive as denying the inextricable connection between bisexuals' oppression and lesbian and gay oppression.

A bisexual is, then, 100 percent lesbian or gay *and* 100 percent heterosexual. Like someone of mixed racial or ethnic heritage, we are simultaneous, full members of both groups. No activity or belief secures our standing; we can stop searching for hospitality. Every place is our home. Each aspect of being a lesbian, gay man, or heterosexual fully applies to every bisexual: We can reclaim all the richness of each community as our own, and we can name and recover from every injury we have withstood as members of both groups. If we attempt a detour around complete pride or healing, we are settling for less than becoming our whole selves.

A bisexual identity brings with it all the components of lesbian, gay, and heterosexual identity, plus the distinctive results of blending both experiences. The oppression and internalized oppression of a bisexual has particular twists and emphasis. For example, gay men and lesbians may be labeled "de-

Bisexuality: The Myths Versus the Truths

S exuality runs along a continuum. It is not a static "thing" but rather a process that can flow, changing throughout our lifetime. Bisexuality falls along this continuum. As Boston bisexual activist Robyn Ochs says, bisexuality is the "potential for being sexually and/or romantically involved with members of either gender."

MYTH: Bisexuals are promiscuous/swingers.

TRUTH: Bisexual people have a range of sexual behaviors. Some have multiple partners; some have one partner; some go through partnerless periods. Promiscuity is no more prevalent in the bisexual population than in other groups of people.

MYTH: Bisexuals are equally attracted to both sexes.

TRUTH: Bisexuals tend to favor either the same or the opposite sex, while recognizing their attraction to both genders.

MYTH: Bisexual means having concurrent lovers of both genders.

TRUTH: Bisexual simply means the *potential* for involvement with either gender. This may mean sexually, emotionally, in reality, or in fantasy. Some bisexual people may have concurrent lovers; others may relate to different genders at various time periods. Most bisexuals do not need to see both genders in order to feel fulfilled.

MYTH: Bisexuals cannot be monogamous.

TRUTH: Bisexuality is a sexual orientation. It is inde-

viant," while bisexuals may be labeled "exotic." Bisexuals, gay
men, and lesbians all generally internalize "not feeling safe" in
the world, which may, for example, produce overdiversifica-

pendent of a lifestyle of monogamy or nonmonogamy. Bisexuals are as capable as anyone of making a long-term
monogamous commitment to a partner they love. Bisexuals live a variety of lifestyles, as do gays and heterosexuals.

MYTH: Bisexuals are denying their lesbianism or gayness.

TRUTH: Bisexuality is a legitimate sexual orientation
which incorporates gayness. Most bisexuals consider themselves part of the generic term "gay." Many are quite active
in the gay community, both socially and politically. Some
of us use terms such as "bisexual lesbian" to increase our
visibility on both issues.

MYTH: Bisexuals are in "transition."

TRUTH: Some people go through a transitional period
of bisexuality on their way to adopting a lesbian/gay or
heterosexual identity. For many others, bisexuality remains
a long-term orientation. Indeed, we are finding that homosexuality may be a transitional phase in the coming-out
process for bisexual people. . . .

It is important to remember that *bisexual, gay, lesbian,* and
heterosexual are labels created by a homophobic, biphobic,
heterosexist society to separate and alienate us from each
other. We are all unique; we don't fit into neat little categories. We sometimes need to use these labels for political
reasons and to increase our visibilities. Our sexual esteem
is facilitated by acknowledging and accepting the differences and seeing the beauty in our diversity.

"Myths/Realities of Bisexuality," *Bi Any Other Name: Bisexual People Speak Out*. Eds.
Loraine Hutchins and Lani Kaahumanu. Boston: Alyson Publications, 1991.

tion for bisexuals: taking on multiple careers, social change projects, etc. For lesbians and gay men, this segment may produce a different version of the same unsure stance, a constriction of life options: accepting narrow, limited possibilities for careers, social change projects, etc. Bisexuals can play the fullest role possible by claiming every portion of our identity and leading in the subversion of oppression wherever we go and with each person with whom we come into contact. Just as someone with one Israeli parent and one Palestinian parent has a profound potential role with Israelis, with Palestinians, and with others of the same mixed background, an immense opportunity awaits us as bisexuals.

BISEXUAL LIBERATION AND WOMEN'S LIBERATION

All oppressions operate in complex relationship to one another, each insuring the perpetuation of the other. Because the oppression of bisexuals, like all lesbian and gay oppression, is used to reinforce sexism in our society by creating a penalty for challenging gender roles, our liberation is particularly tied to women's liberation. Any liberation work we undertake as bisexuals must incorporate a commitment to ending sexism. To assert that our liberation could be considered separate from feminism would create the same kind of false and destructive division as considering our liberation separate from lesbian and gay liberation. Bisexual women's organizations have consistently backed feminist policies and activities, and bisexual women generally conceive their identities in the context of women's liberation. Bisexual women's continued dedication to women's liberation and the dissolution of gender roles, the continued advancement of bisexual men's understanding of and participation in this same effort, and joint work on the elimination of sexism in mixed-gender bisexual groups is essential to the success of bisexual liberation.

We are emerging from the initial stages of bisexual liberation work and have a unique opportunity to devise a strategy based on the victories and errors of past and current liberation movements. By delineating two distinct and substantially disparate programs for bisexual liberation, I hope to help frame a discussion of a full range of possible strategies.

1. *Build a bisexual liberation movement by founding and building local, regional, national, and international bisexual organizations.*

Many bisexuals advocate forging a bisexual movement that aims to create visibility, spread information about bisexuality, draw as many people as possible into the identity, offer a safe place for anyone who takes on the identity, organize social events for bisexuals, take political action against bisexual oppression, and continually grow in membership. This plan, modeled on many other liberation movements, could inspire a ground swell of bisexual comings out, bring the term "bisexual" into common usage and raise bisexuality into routine recognition as a sexual identity, foster personal and collective pride among bisexuals, and document and address instances of mistreatment of bisexuals by heterosexuals and lesbians and gay men. Through this plan, large numbers of people could be exposed to the concept of a third option for sexual identity, sexual activity, and affection.

Central to this strategy is an assumption that many people will take on a bisexual identity as the identity becomes more visible and less stigmatized, and that drawing people into the identity is desirable and furthers our liberation. Currently, very small numbers of people label themselves "bisexual," though large numbers of people have sexual feelings or fantasies about or contact with both women and men at some point in their lives. As we chart the course of our work, we must ask ourselves if selecting this plan and thereby proliferating the identity among this latter group would assist in the elimination of the oppression or simply offer us the feeling of comfort that we are not isolated in our experience. We must learn to distinguish between a personal and political belief that all people are capable of emotional, physical, and sexual closeness with both genders, and chauvinism that places bisexuality over other sexual identities.

To organize separately as bisexuals may imply an acceptance

of the societal assumption that "heterosexual" and "lesbian and gay" are *real* categories of human beings, that we need a third such category in order to assert our own brand of hegemony [a prevailing culture's dominance and influence over others]. Bisexuals could meet in organizations and only commiserate about feelings of marginalization and homelessness, while simultaneously touting our "superiority," leaving us caught in internalized oppression and playing a role that helps to perpetuate lesbian and gay oppression. The current system relies on the segregation of heterosexuals and lesbians and gay men. If we proceed with a plan which asserts a hegemonous third category, we risk trivialization, division from the other two, and further ghettoizing our efforts.

In addition, to identify bisexuality as discrete from heterosexuality and homosexuality may lead to the misinterpretation that sexual closeness with both women and men is relegated to bisexuals only. If it is assumed that only heterosexuals are free to get close to a member of the other gender, and lesbians and gay men are the only ones who are free to get close to a member of the same gender, then forming a bisexual movement could compound these absurd divisions.

On the other hand, if bisexuality is defined as the potential to have sexual relationships with women and/or men, then ubiquitously offering the identity and welcoming all people into it could unleash the full continuum of human possibilities. Given the weight of lesbian and gay oppression, that process could be quite lengthy. But by slowly bringing everyone into one identity that holds infinite options, the whole system of identification and oppression would inevitably collapse.

The key difficulty of this strategy appears to be the potential for divisiveness between those who identify as bisexuals and those who do not, while the key strength may be the achievement of visibility of the identity.

2. Build bisexual organizations for the sole purpose of generating small support groups and take political action against the oppression of bisexuals only as a constituency within the lesbian and gay liberation movement.

Support group meeting topics could include what has been good and what has been hard about being bisexual, coming-out stories, specific aspects of internalized oppression, setting goals for our lives and leadership, and visions of a future without oppression. There, bisexuals would reclaim pride, tell stories, and give voice to the pain of mistreatment in an atmosphere of warmth and safety. Support groups generally work best when a leader assists participants to take turns talking about their lives, and when there is an agreement to meet for a specified number of weeks or months.

In addition, group members could discuss their experiences as lesbians and gay men and as heterosexuals. Meetings might then address what's been good and hard about being lesbian and gay and heterosexual, and specific topics such as "handling sexism in relationships with members of the other gender," or "how lesbian and gay oppression affects us at work." If support groups remain focused on "bisexual oppression," we may not wholly dismantle our internalized oppression. By examining all the interlocking parts of our oppression, we could begin to imagine coming into our real selves outside all oppression, no longer inside the box of any identity.

These support groups would welcome anyone who identifies as bisexual. No one would be "recruited" to a group or to the identity based on a sexual attraction they "once had." Thus, support groups would be designed for the relatively small number of people who identify themselves as bisexuals and have experienced the accompanying oppression and internalization of oppression.

If bisexual political and social activities were narrowed to the formation of support groups, bisexuals could isolate themselves within the sanctuary of their groups without ever taking on liberation work. As long as lesbian, gay, and bisexual oppression exists, we may be pulled to withdraw into corners and closets that appear to be safe.

Political leadership would include working in lesbian and gay organizations to quash lesbian, gay, and bisexual oppression, and founding and building heterosexual organizations which fight to end that oppression (such as Parents and Friends of Lesbians and Gays—PFLAG). A bisexual could select either approach based on her or his history with identity, relationships, community, and social change work. Bolstered by our participation in support groups, bisexual activists could make personal decisions about where and when to come out based not on shame or fear but on her or his best thinking about how to be most influential and self-respecting in each situation. This plan requires that bisexuals bar internalized oppression from bearing on those decisions but risks burying bisexuals in lesbian, gay, and heterosexual organizations where they may never feel safe in assuming a proud stance as these organizations' rightful leaders.

A UNITED COALITION

Underlying this plan is an assumption that bisexuals' political energies are more strategically useful if applied to the lesbian and gay liberation movement than to an independent bisexual movement. If this assumption is correct, then people with, for instance, one Asian parent and one white parent would best caucus in support groups with other Amer-Asians to find pride in and empathy for their unique experience. Then, rooted in that identity, they would choose to be activists on behalf of the elimination of racism in organizations of Asians, of people of color, and of white people, rather than creating an Amer-Asian liberation movement.

In addition, by emphasizing lesbian and gay liberation, this strategy aims to expose a continuum of sexuality and affection, instead of making a third sexual identity more available by centering on bisexual visibility. As we gradually dismantled internalized oppression through support groups, bisexuals could become models of the flexible use of identity. And as we gradually put an end to lesbian and gay oppression, each sexual identity could be eliminated one by one and replaced with acceptance of our infinite human diversity. In the meantime, handling mistreatment in lesbian and gay and heterosexual groups would be difficult for many of us. Bisexuals' internalized oppression could turn this vision into an excuse for publicly and privately denying who we are.

This strategy could give bisexuals access to the affirmation and healing we need to prepare to claim our homes among lesbians and gay men and heterosexuals and rapidly take our place with them as powerful leaders of all people. By establishing the whole of bisexual liberation work within lesbian and gay liberation and heterosexual organizations, the joint power of the resulting coalition could exert tremendous force against the oppression.

The key difficulty of this strategy appears to be the potential for bisexuals to remain hidden out of fear, while the key strength may be a unified coalition on behalf of lesbian, gay, and bisexual liberation.

WE MUST END OPPRESSION BASED ON SEXUAL IDENTITY AND GENDER

Appraising the accuracy of the theoretical underpinnings of these two programs, and their likely strengths and difficulties in practice, is a demanding and complex task. Just as difficult is imagining and deliberating on every potential option before us. Our challenge is to take into account every aspect of the current state of bisexual liberation, every piece of information we can assemble about what has worked and what has not in this and all liberation struggles, and every implication of selecting each possible program for action. This work calls us to transcend the oppression and internalized oppression that can easily sabotage our thinking and our actions.

We must constantly re-evaluate what is most effective to liberate bisexuals, and standing on that foundation, we will successfully abolish all oppression based on sexual identity and gender.

The Need for a Centralized Movement Remains

MARSHALL KIRK AND HUNTER MADSEN

In the following excerpt, Marshall Kirk and Hunter Madsen offer their brief analysis of the contemporary gay rights movement, focusing in particular on the lack of a single national organization that could focus activists' energies toward a clearer set of common goals. Though written in 1989, the authors' observations continue to ring true: "Given the diffuseness of gay power and the chaotic state of gay organization, it's no wonder that our meager advances have come primarily in scattered localities, and that our community's stature on the national political stage has been abysmally low."

Kirk, a neuropsychiatry researcher, logician, and poet, collaborated with Madsen, a public communications expert, on After the Ball: How America Will Conquer Its Hatred and Fear of Homosexuals in the '90s, *which is considered a significant examination of the contemporary gay rights movement.*

The throne of national leadership is not without its many pretenders, both individual and organizational: that much is plain. Anyone asking a gay hotline to connect him with 'the national gay organization' will be directed, depending on the locale, to any of the following: the National Gay and Lesbian Task Force (NGLTF), the Fund for Human Dignity (which split from NGLTF in 1986), the Human Rights Campaign Fund (HRCF) (which swallowed the insolvent Gay Rights National Lobby that same year), the National Gay Rights Advocates, the Lambda Legal Defense and Education Fund, the

National Coalition of Black Lesbians and Gays, and, in recent years, the new AIDS empires of GMHC (Gay Men's Health Crisis), the AIDS Action Council, and others.

Some of these 'national' organizations acknowledge the specificity of their missions in their names. Yet even those groups with general-sounding names turn out, upon inquiry, to concern themselves chiefly with some particular aspect of gay advocacy—political lobbying, legal defense, public education, gay health protection, advancement of women's rights, etc.—and not with the guidance of the movement as a whole. There is *no* central institution, no gay equivalent of the National Association for the Advancement of Colored People.

Certainly, the talented and ambitious leaders of the quasi-national gay groups might each *like* to be Queen of the Realm (or perhaps Pope of Greenwich Village), but none has been allowed to accede by the rest. Indeed, our organizations are locked in a fratricidal struggle for members and dollars—that is, for their very survival. They take frequent swipes at one another in the gay press. The movement's leaders are inclined to trace this bureaucratic caterwauling, like everything else, back to "internalized homophobia," because—explains Jeff Levi, the executive director of NGLTF—"We're more willing to attack one another than to go after our common enemy." But a more plausible motive is old-fashioned *Realpolitik* [practical politics]. As Humpty Dumpty observed, "The only question is, which is to be master—that's all." Hearing a dozen different answers to Humpty's question is no answer at all.

A UNITED NATIONS WITHOUT A GENERAL ASSEMBLY

Given the diffuseness of gay power and the chaotic state of gay organization, it's no wonder that our meager advances have come primarily in scattered localities, and that our community's stature on the national political stage has been abysmally low.

This must change. There should be *one* national gay organization, universally known as such. That organization should have coordinated task forces dedicated to political lobbying, legal action, gay life (i.e., the protection and enrichment of gay society and culture), health issues, and public education. It should represent gay men and women, young and old, of every race and religion. The organization should link up local branches in every city and hamlet in the country and be able to direct its national resources at specific regional targets as needed. Membership and regular donations should be strongly encouraged by local branches.

As trade unions (pointedly, the AFL–CIO [American Federation of Labor and Congress of Industrial Organizations]) learned many years ago, there is tremendous strength in unification under a single, well-run organization. The need for such is obvious to everyone in the gay community except those activists with a personal stake in the status quo. Yet activists remain entrenched in their fiefdoms. Consequently, we're left with a movement that resembles the United Nations without a General Assembly: a loose handful of weak specialized agencies, claiming as members many hundreds of local 'grass roots' groups that never come together to caucus. Or, to put it another way, gay organization in this country is a wagon wheel with an extensive rim, a snaggle-toothed arrangement of frail national spokes, and no hub at all.

CHAPTER 5

VOICES FROM
THE MOVEMENT

AMERICAN
SOCIAL
MOVEMENTS

I Have No Brothers: How Women Fared in the Early Movement

Del Martin

In 1955, Del Martin and Phyllis Lyon founded the Daughters of Bilitis (DOB), the first lesbian organization in the United States. They believed, as did DOB members, that gay men did not recognize lesbians' concerns but expected their full support in a movement that lacked female leadership. Martin and Lyon were the first to challenge this exclusion; however, their challenge would not last.

In the following selection, Martin reveals her frustration on all fronts—political, social, legal, and spiritual—within the early gay rights movement and announces her withdrawal from both the gay rights movement and community: "There is no hate in this good-bye—only the bitter sting of disappointment."

After fifteen years of working for the homophile movement—of mediating, counselling, appeasing, of working for coalition and unity—I am facing a very real identity crisis. Like NACHO [North American Conference on Homophile Organizations] I have been torn apart. I am bereft. For I have during this week of struggle between the men and the women, the conservatives and the Gay Liberationists, been forced to the realization that I have no brothers in the homophile movement.

Oh yes, when six of my sisters from the Daughters of Bilitis, Nova and Gay Women's Liberation stood with me to confront the NACHO meeting on August 26th (the day of the National Women's Strike in 1970) about the relevance of the homophile movement to the women within it, the delegates passed a resolution in support of the women's liberation movement. They rationalized that all of their organizations were open to women, but the women didn't join in numbers and they just didn't know what else they could do to relate to their Lesbian sisters. We suggested that their programs and their publications were not inclusive of or relevant to women. They decried the segregationist organizations which we represented, but would not address themselves to the underlying reason for the existence of separate women's organizations—that the female homosexual faces sex discrimination not only in the heterosexual world, but within the homophile community.

And so, like my sister, [poet and journalist] Robin Morgan, I have come to the conclusion that I must say, "Good Bye to All That." Goodbye to the wasteful, meaningless verbiage of empty resolutions made by hollow men of self-proclaimed privilege. They neither speak for us nor to us. They acknowledged us on our "day" and then ditched us that very same night in their "male only" sanctuaries. It's the system, and there was not one among them with guts enough to put a stop to it. And, too late, they shall find that the joke is really on them.

Goodbye, my alienated brothers. Goodbye to the male chauvinists of the homophile movement who are so wrapped up in the "cause" they espouse that they have lost sight of the people for whom the cause came into being. Goodbye to the bulwark of the Mattachine (Society) grandfathers, self-styled monarchs of a youth cult which is no longer theirs. As they cling to their old ideas and their old values in a time that calls for radical change, I must bid them farewell. There is so much to be done, and I have neither the stomach nor the inclination to stand by and watch them self destruct.

Goodbye to co-ed organizations like SIR. The Political Action Dinner, we were told, was a "community" project. The Society for Individual Rights supposedly had finally learned that politics isn't a loner's game and called out the forces of coalition in the gay community. The Daughters of Bilitis responded, came to the first planning committee meetings and were, as usual, overlooked as plans progressed. Better it should be a SIR blow job. And it was.

Goodbye to all that. The finale at the head table said it all. It was no oversight. It was a demonstration of where the head is at—not just one man's head, for he was representative of the vast majority of those men present. Women are invisible. There is only one credential for acceptance in the homophile "brotherhood"—the handle [San Francisco] Mayor [Joseph L.] Alioto couldn't find on Women's Day.

Goodbye, not just to SIR, but all those homophile organizations across the country with an open door policy for women. It's only window dressing for the public, and in the small towns of suburbia, for mutual protection. It doesn't really mean anything and smacks of paternalism. Goodbye, too, (temporarily, I trust) to my sisters who demean themselves by accepting "women's status" in these groups—making and serving the coffee, doing the secretarial work, soothing the brows of the policy makers who tell them, "We're doing it all for you, too." Don't believe it, sisters, for you are only an afterthought that never took place.

Goodbye to *Vector* [SIR's monthly magazine]. Goodbye to the "Police Beat"—the defense of wash room sex and pornographic movies. That was never my bag anyway. Goodbye to the Women's Page and the NACHO delegate who admitted that's how he regarded my column, professing all the while, of course, that he considered it most worthwhile reading. He meant it as a compliment. Goodbye to my editor, George Mendanhall, who has tried to understand and who is seeking to cement relations between the men and women of the community. He can't go it alone. So I say, "Go ahead, George. Let it all hang out. It's all they have, and *that* needs to be exposed."

Goodbye to all the "representative" homophile publications that look more like magazines for male nudist colonies. Goodbye to the biased male point of view. The editors say they have encouraged women to contribute, but they don't. Nor will they until the format is changed, policy broadened and their material taken seriously.

Goodbye to the gay bars that discriminate against women. Goodbye to those that "allow" them in only if they dress up in skirts, while the men slop around in their "queer" costumes. Gay Liberationists are right when they observe that gay bars ghettoize the homophile community. They are, after all, our chief base for socialization, for meeting *people* of our own kind. But there is no time or place for forming friendships, for exchanging ideas, for camaraderie—only for dispensing of drinks and sex partners.

Goodbye to the Hallowe'en Balls, the drag shows and parties. It was fun, while it lasted. But the humor has gone out of the game. The exaggeration of the switching (or swishing) of sex roles has become the norm in the public eye. While we were laughing at ourselves we became the laughing stock and lost the personhood we were seeking. It is time to stop mimicking the heterosexual society we've been trying to escape. It is time to get our heads together to find out *who we really are.*

Goodbye to NACHO. It never really happened. It was a non-organization consisting only of reams of purple dittoed rules and regulations that no one had the time nor stamina to read and big-mouthed, self-appointed and anointed homophile leaders—the steeple without the people.

Goodbye to Gay Liberation Front (GLF), too. They applauded the Lesbians who wished to establish common cause with them and the other men at the NACHO meeting. But somehow we are left with the feeling their applause was for the disruption of the meeting, not its purpose. There is reason for the splits within their own movement, why there is a women's caucus in GLF in New York and why there is a Gay Women's Liberation in the San Francisco Bay Area. Like the tired old men they berate they have not come to grips with the gut issues. Until they do, *their* revolution cannot be ours. Their liberation would only further enslave us.

Goodbye to the various Councils on Religion and the Homosexual (CRH). Like the institutions they sprang from they are bastions of male prestige—male evangelists from two disparate worlds. There is no place for women in the Christian and homophile brotherhoods. Be warned, my sisters, CRH spells only purgatory for you.

Goodbye to the male homophile community. "Gay is good," but not good enough—so long as it is limited to white males only. We joined with you in what we mistakenly thought was a common cause. A few of you tried, we admit. But you are still too few, and even you fall short of the mark. You, too, are victims of our culture. Fifteen years of masochism is enough. None of us is getting any younger or any closer to where it's really at. So, regretfully, I must say goodbye to you, too. It's been nice and all that, but I have work to do. My friends neither look up to me nor down at me. They face me as equals, and we interact reciprocally with respect and love.

There is no hate in this goodbye—only the bitter sting of disappointment. Momentarily I am pregnant with rage at your blindness and your deafness—the psychosomatic symptoms of narcissism and egocentricity. But my rage will pass. Most of it has been spent already. For I realize you were programmed by society for your role of supremacy. But somehow I expected more of you. I had hoped that you were my brothers and would grow up, to recognize that freedom is not self contained. You cannot be free until you free me—*and all women*—until you become aware that, in all the roles and games you play, *you* are always "*IT.*"

Believe it or not, there is love, too, in this farewell—just as there has always been. How could anyone hold a grudge against helpless beings who are compelled to grope for their very existence? But I must leave you—for your good as well as mine. I refuse to be your scapegoat. By removing the target, you may no longer mock me. Besides, I must go where the action is—where there is still hope, where there is possibility for personal and collective growth. It is a revelation to find acceptance, equality, love and friendship—everything we sought in the homophile community—not there, but in the women's movement.

I will not be your "nigger" any longer. Nor was I ever your mother. Those were stultifying roles you laid on me, and I shall no longer concern myself with your toilet training. You're in the big leagues now, and we're both playing for big stakes. They didn't turn out to be the same.

As I bid you adieu, I leave each of you to your own device. Take care of it, stroke it gently, mouth it and fondle it. As the center of your consciousness, it's really all you have.

We Need Gay Leaders in Office

HARVEY MILK

In 1977, Harvey Milk won a seat on the San Francisco Board of Supervisors, becoming the first openly gay elected city official. He fought passionately to protect the civil rights of his constituents and felt an enormous sense of responsibility toward the gay community: "A gay person in office can set a tone, can command respect not only from the larger community, but from the young people in our own community who need both examples and hope."

Milk delivered the following speech to the gay caucus of the California Democratic Council on March 10, 1978. It is a well-known example of his skill as a spur-of-the-moment speaker; Milk often used no notes, so the following is a transcription from a tape recording of the event.

M y name is Harvey Milk and I'm here to recruit you. I've been saving this one for years. It's a political joke. I can't help it—I've got to tell it. I've never been able to talk to this many political people before, so if I tell you nothing else you may be able to go home laughing a bit.

This ocean liner was going across the ocean and it sank. And there was one little piece of wood floating and three people swam to it and they realized only one person could hold on to it. So they had a little debate about which was the person. It so happened the three people were the Pope, the President, and Mayor [Richard J.] Daley. The Pope said he was titular head of one of the great religions of the world and he was spiritual adviser to many, many millions and he went on and pontificated and they thought it was a good argument.

Then the President said he was leader of the largest and most powerful nation of the world. What takes place in this country affects the whole world and they thought that was a good argument. And Mayor Daley said he was mayor of the backbone of the United States and what took place in Chicago affected the world, and what took place in the archdiocese of Chicago affected Catholicism. And they thought that was a good argument. So they did it the democratic way and voted. And Daley won, seven to two.

About six months ago, Anita Bryant [singer and conservative activist] in her speaking to God said that the drought in California was because of the gay people. On November 9, the day after I got elected, it started to rain. On the day I got sworn in, we walked to City Hall and it was kinda nice, and as soon as I said the word "I do," it started to rain again. It's been raining since then and the people of San Francisco figure the only way to stop it is to do a recall petition. That's a local joke.

CONSERVATIVES ARE NOT GAINING POLITICAL UPPER HAND

So much for that. Why are we here? Why are gay people here? And what's happening? What's happening to me is the antithesis of what you read about in the papers and what you hear about on the radio. You hear about and read about this movement to the right. That we must band together and fight back this movement to the right. And I'm here to go ahead and say that what you hear and read is what they want you to think because it's not happening. The major media in this country has talked about the movement to the right so much that they've got even us thinking that way. Because they want the legislators to think that there is indeed a movement to the right and that the Congress and the legislators and the city councils will start to move to the right the way the major media want them. So they keep on talking about this move to the right.

So let's look at 1977 and see if there was indeed a move to the right. In 1977, gay people had their rights taken away from them in Miami [because of Bryant's successful campaign to overturn a Miami-Dade County ordinance banning discrimination based on sexual orientation]. But you must remember that in the week before Miami and the week after that, the word homosexual or gay appeared in every single newspaper in this nation in articles both pro and con. In every radio station, in every TV station and every household. For the first time in the history of the world, everybody was talking about it, good or bad. Unless you have dialogue, unless you open the walls of dialogue, you can never reach to change people's opinion. In those two weeks, more good and bad, but *more* about the word homosexual and gay was written than probably in the history of mankind. Once you have dialogue starting, you know you can break down the prejudice. In 1977 we saw a dialogue start. In 1977, we saw a gay person [Milk] elected in San Francisco. In 1977 we saw the state of Mississippi decriminalize marijuana. In 1977, we saw the convention [for women's rights] of conventions in Houston. And I want to know where the movement to the right is happening.

What that is is a record of what happened last year. What we must do is make sure that 1978 continues the movement that is really happening that the media don't want you to know about, that is the movement to the left. It's up to California Democratic Council (CDC) to put the pressures on Sacramento—not to just bring flowers to Sacramento—but to break down the walls and the barriers so the movement to the left continues and progress continues in the nation. We have before us coming up several issues we must speak out on. Probably the most important issue outside the Briggs [Initiative to bar gays from teaching in public schools in California]—which we will come to—but we do know what will take place this June [the initiative was defeated]. We know there's an issue on the ballot called Jarvis-Gann [a tax relief measure that critics feared would sap local governments of property tax revenue, threatening the survival of local businesses and service industries]. We hear the taxpayers talk about it on both sides. But what you don't hear is that it's probably the most racist issue on the ballot in a long time. In the city and county of San Francisco, if it passes and we indeed have to lay off people, who will they be? The last in, not the first in, and who are the last in but the minorities? Jarvis-Gann is a racist issue. We must address that issue. We must not talk away from it. We must not allow them to talk about the money it's going to save, because look at who's going to save the money and who's going to get hurt.

We also have another issue that we've started in some of the north counties and I hope in some of the south counties it continues. In San Francisco elections we're asking—at least we hope to ask—that the U.S. government put pressure on the closing of the South African consulate. That must happen. There is a major difference between an embassy in Washington which is a diplomatic bureau, and a consulate in major cities. A consulate is there for one reason only—to promote business, economic gains, tourism, investment. And every time you have business going to South Africa, you're promoting a regime that's offensive [and did not end until the 1990s].

In the city of San Francisco, if everyone of 51 percent of that city were to go to South Africa, they would be treated as second-class citizens. That is an offense to the people of San Francisco and I hope all my colleagues up there will take every step we can to close down that consulate and hope that people in other parts of the state follow us in that lead. The battles must be started some place and CDC is the greatest place to start the battles.

WE NEED GAY LEADERSHIP

I know we are pressed for time so I'm going to cover just one more little point. That is to understand why it is important that gay people run for office and that gay people get elected. I know there are many people in this room who are running for central committee who are gay. I encourage you. There's a major reason why. If my non-gay friends and supporters in this room understand it, they'll probably understand why I've run so often before I finally made it. Y'see right now, there's a controversy going on in this convention about the governor. Is he speaking out enough? Is he strong enough for gay rights? And there is a controversy and for us to say it is not would be fool-ish. Some people are satisfied and some people are not.

You see there is a major difference—and it remains a vital difference—between a friend and a gay person, a friend in of-fice and a gay person in office. Gay people have been slandered nationwide. We've been tarred and we've been brushed with the picture of pornography. In Dade County [Florida], we were accused of child molestation. It's not enough anymore just to have friends represent us. No matter how good that friend may be.

The black community made up its mind to that a long time ago. That the myths against blacks can only be dispelled by electing black leaders, so the black community could be judged by the leaders and not by the myths or black crimi-nals. The Spanish community must not be judged by Latin criminals or myths. The Asian community must not be judged by Asian criminals or myths. The Italian community should not be judged by the mafia, myths. And the time has come when the gay community must not be judged by our criminals and myths.

Like every other group, we must be judged by our leaders and by those who are themselves gay, those who are visible. For invisible, we remain in limbo—a myth, a person with no parents, no brothers, no sisters, no friends who are straight, no important positions in employment. A tenth of a nation sup-posedly composed of stereotypes and would-be seducers of children—and no offense meant to the stereotypes. But today, the black community is not judged by its friends, but by its black legislators and leaders. And we must give people the chance to judge us by our leaders and legislators. A gay per-son in office can set a tone, can command respect not only from the larger community, but from the young people in our own community who need both examples and hope.

WE MUST GIVE PEOPLE HOPE

The first gay people we elect must be strong. They must not be content to sit in the back of the bus. They must not be content to accept pablum. They must be above wheeling and dealing. They must be—for the good of all of us—independent, unbought. The anger and the frustrations that some of us feel is because we are misunderstood, and friends can't feel that anger and frustration. They can sense it in us, but they can't feel it. Because a friend has never gone through what is known as coming out. I will never forget what it was like coming out and having nobody to look up toward. I remember the lack of hope—and our friends can't fulfill that.

I can't forget the looks on faces of people who've lost hope. Be they gay, be they seniors, be they blacks looking for an almost-impossible job, be they Latins trying to explain their problems and aspirations in a tongue that's foreign to them. I personally will never forget that people are more important than buildings. I use the word "I" because I'm proud. I stand here tonight in front of my gay sisters, brothers and friends because I'm proud of you. I think it's time that we have many legislators who are gay and proud of that fact and do not have to remain in the closet. I think that a gay person, up-front, will not walk away from a responsibility and be afraid of being tossed out of office. After Dade County, I walked among the angry and the frustrated night after night and I looked at their faces. And in San Francisco, three days before Gay Pride Day, a person was killed just because he was gay. And that night, I walked among the sad and the frustrated at City Hall in San Francisco and later that night as they lit candles on Castro Street and stood in silence, reaching out for some symbolic thing that would give them hope. These were strong people, people whose faces I knew from the shop, the streets, meetings and people who I never saw before but I knew. They were strong, but even they needed hope.

And the young gay people in the Altoona, Pennsylvanias, and the Richmond, Minnesotas, who are coming out and hear Anita Bryant on television and her story. The only thing they have to look forward to is hope. And you have to give them hope. Hope for a better world, hope for a better tomorrow, hope for a better place to come to if the pressures at home are too great. Hope that all will be all right. Without hope, not only gays, but the blacks, the seniors, the handicapped, the us'es, the us'es will give up. And if you help elect to the central committee and other offices, more gay people, that gives a green light to all who feel disenfranchised, a green light to move forward. It means hope to a nation that has given up, because if a gay person makes it, the doors are open to everyone.

So if there is a message I have to give, it is that if I've found one overriding thing about my personal election, it's the fact that if a gay person can be elected, it's a green light. And you and you and you, you have to give people hope. Thank you very much.

A Gay Rights Activist Reflects on the Movement

LARRY KRAMER

In the 1980s, Larry Kramer—novelist, playwright, and gay rights activist—helped found the Gay Men's Health Crisis (GMHC) in response to the growing AIDS epidemic, which first hit the gay community in the United States. Near the end of the decade, however, he had become disillusioned with the GMHC's waning aggressiveness in fighting the government and pharmaceutical companies to release more effective treatments more quickly. In 1987, he left the GMHC and founded the AIDS Coalition to Unleash Power (ACT UP), an ad hoc community protest group that exerted enormous influence over the development of treatments, the release of more effective drugs, and the funding of community services.

Then one day, Kramer observes, "in the middle of fighting this plague and proving to ourselves and to the world that we could work together and fight together in a more-or-less unified fashion, the fighting stopped."

In the following speech, delivered at the University of Wisconsin in February 1999, Kramer reflects on his life as an activist and attempts to discover why the fighting stopped. He despairs for the future, especially given the continuing presence of AIDS, the seeming recklessness of the younger gay generations and the nebulous network of organizations fighting among themselves instead of fighting for gay rights and gay survival.

I live in a house on a hill. It overlooks a lake. My lover, who is a very fine and gentle and caring man, built it for us. Where we live is far from traffic and very quiet. I am free to think and

Larry Kramer, "Yesterday, Today, and Tomorrow," www.advocate.com, March 1999. Copyright © 1999 by *The Advocate*. Reproduced by permission of the author.

VOICES FROM THE MOVEMENT • 175

read and write. I have little to obstruct my view of beauty and happiness but memory. I try to gain some understanding of why I am still here and where I have been. Why is it important for me to understand so many things that are probably impossible to understand? I can only answer that this is my way: This is the only way I know how to deal with my memory, which is filled to overflowing with the history of gay people and the history of AIDS. I find that the longer I remain alive, the more I feel the obligation to try to understand why I have been spared and so many of whom I grew up with have not.

I wonder now what I expected being an older gay man would be like—what I would be like—when I first accepted the fact, some 40 or so years ago, that I would be a gay man, that is: live my life openly as one. I guess no kid ever sees himself becoming an old fart. I had dreamed a lot about a few things—finding a wonderful man and living in a lovely house; I always wanted both of these, and I have them, so some dreams really can come true. I didn't want to become an old fart, and I hope I've made that come true too: I didn't want to become anything like most of the straight men who were, and are, supposed to be role models and rarely are. I don't think I'm anything like most straight men, and I take pride in that. Straight men, as a rule, have not been very role model-y.

Did I in any way wonder what bridges I was burning or where the bridges I was crossing over would lead to?

I didn't expect to become an activist. That's for certain. I was on my way to being a screenwriter—a comedy writer— perhaps someday a playwright. My mom, who loved the theater, was pretty role model-y; she wanted me to write plays, and I did.

I didn't expect a plague.

But it came, and a bunch of us, not a great many of us, enlisted in an army to fight it.

That's how I became part of the gay movement. Which is very different from just being a gay man. And if I hadn't given much thought to what I might be expecting as a gay man, I certainly had no idea what it would be like being in the gay movement. I guess I'm still in the gay movement. I'm gay. I'm writing this. I write about only gay and AIDS stuff.

I do feel I have a responsibility as an openly gay man who has made some sort of name for himself to show my face and be a role model for gay kids desperately in need of them. I know when I was a kid I sure would have liked to have heard a few guys like me tell me how to get from there to here.

But something happens when you get older. It's not that I feel too old or don't have enough energy or have lost interest in our causes and our goals. It's not that everyone else is so much younger, although I do indeed wonder what happens to all the gays once they get past a certain age. They seem to disappear. At least I haven't quite done that.

And it's not that I don't have empathy with those now fighting our fights and fighting them, what's more, as if they're new ones. No, that's not why I feel I'm not still in the gay movement.

What happens is this: One day you realize that all the fights are the same fights. It may be a different cast of characters, but they're the same fights. This organization is doing a terrible job (which it probably is). That organization is invading our turf (which it probably is). Another bunch is doing such and so. We do tend to fight among ourselves on a very petty level. The map of the gay community is about as Balkanized as Eastern Europe. In the outside world gays win one battle and lose a dozen. They love us, and they hate us, and depending on which poll, we can slit our wrists or modestly celebrate. After a while the good news isn't as exciting and the bad news hurts even more.

So what happens (and it happens, I'm told, to older folks in general) is—as that revoltingly accurate slang expression puts it—you can't get it up anymore. It becomes increasingly difficult to get excited, yet again, about all the things that got me so hot and sweaty when I was younger.

By the time you reach 63 you just don't feel very inspirational anymore. It's very sad to come face-to-face with the horrid truth that many things never change. Many people think that things are better for people of color or for women or for gays, and I say to you, Hey, this country is over 200 years old, and this world is many thousands of years old, and I would not call what we have achieved during such a long time very much progress. I've become very conscious as I read so much history in my library overlooking our lake that there's another murder like Matthew Shepard's happening somewhere with alarming regularity. [Shepard was robbed, beaten, and left to die in Laramie, WY, after it was discovered that he was gay.] In 17th century Holland they got rid of gay kids by tossing them into the water, weighted down with rocks.

Yes, it's heartbreakingly sad to have to stare at the irrefutable fact that not much progress is ever made. It's also very painful to see that I have been unable to do as much about matters I cared a very great deal about—and still do—as I would have liked to have done—and still want to do.

Gay AIDS activists did manage to effect a few changes, and I should be more generous about them. We learned how to overhaul a hatefully discriminatory and bureaucratic drug-delivery system so that people with HIV (and people with other illnesses too) could live a little longer. Maybe because the plague hasn't gone away, I'm unwilling to celebrate this really historic feat. We just didn't finish the job, and many of us act as if we did. So that's another heavy fact to live with, that feeling that we, and I, didn't finish the job.

One day something very peculiar happened. I can't tell you exactly what day it was. Perhaps you might remember when it was. It just seemed to dawn. One day, in the middle of fighting this plague and proving to ourselves and to the world that we could work together and fight together in a more-or-less unified fashion, the fighting stopped. I couldn't see or hear or feel the gay movement anymore. The world I'd lived in for some 20 years was suddenly very quiet.

And it still is.

Which is odd because the plague hasn't gone away and we still don't have very many rights and we still don't have very many organizations that are any good and we still don't have a way to network with each other. I still can't marry my nice man. If we lived in Texas, the police could barge right into our bedroom in our lovely home and arrest us while we were making love. And, of course, Matthew Shepard's unspeakably brutal murder still gets repeated.

No, I don't feel very inspirational these days. I'm too worried to inspire anyone, especially the younger generations who need it most. I'm too worried about too many gay people believing that things are not so bad these days or wanting to believe that things are not so bad these days.

Polls of college kids still say how much they hate us, and polls of Republicans still say how much they hate us, and polls of anybody still say how much they hate us, and I still can't get articles like this one published in the "mainstream" press.

Why did we stop fighting?

Once upon a time I believed that after our fight to end AIDS was over, all of us who survived this plague (and there have been more and more of us) would build a future. I saw— and I guess the unemployed screenwriter in me must have been writing a fantasy sequence—communities of wise gay men and lesbians, councils of elders, armies of activist survivors, all so overwhelmingly grateful to still be alive, to have escaped infection and death, that they would see to it that what had happened wouldn't happen again. They would build, at last, our gay city on a hill, filled with new buildings built on stronger foundations and filled with the best and the brightest figuring out the smartest ways to take lesbians and gay men to the moon. Rich gay men and women would fund organizations and media and networking of all kinds from coast to coast, from big city to smallest town, all across America. All across the world!

Yes, I genuinely believed this would happen. How could it not? We had been spared from the jaws of death, hadn't we? Had I not seen how gay men and lesbians, when they care enough, when they're frightened enough, can work together in a relatively unselfish fashion? As we came closer and closer, we believed, to the end of one plague, I came more and more to assume that we could and would at last build our beautiful house overlooking the lake.

The other thing I believed was that we'd never forget, we would always honor the dead. A lot of our brothers and sisters, the generations that came before us, our blood kin, died, and we must never for one second forget the fact that each and every one of us is related by blood to every single other gay man and lesbian who not only died from AIDS but who has ever lived.

This is a notion I feel very strongly about. It is also a notion the time for which, I fear, unfortunately has not come.

I still can't believe that so many of us would be forgotten so quickly, so fast.

How do I know our AIDS dead are forgotten? Because so many gay men and lesbians and the gay movement have forgotten AIDS, do not want to remember it is still here, do not believe it will return in fury, and prefer instead to behave in ways, like a matador with a red cape, that will only aggravate its return.

There is always such a great sadness about opportunities lost, moments of possibility that must be grasped before they are blown away by other winds. Perhaps my age, or my virus, has made me overly conscious of time, of the preciousness of each day, of each moment in the arms of my lover, in our beautiful house—I wish everyone the joy of living with someone you love in a place where you are happy.

How can everyone not be aware of how swiftly joys can be taken away? Haven't we learned anything from all the education and experience that we've had? Most of the books I've been reading are history books. The main thing I'm learning from reading them is that we aren't in them. It's hard to believe so many books can be so filled with lies. Because we are not in these histories, in the eyes of most people, especially academics, we therefore don't exist. Therefore few schools teach our history. Therefore no pulpit proclaims and no Congress protects our history. Too many gay historians, as a group, have rather lazily and arbitrarily established that since the word *ho-*

mosexual was not invented until the late 19th century, there is no history for them to write about before that date. This relieves them of the obligation to locate one.

No one has "found" our history. Just as so many gay writers can find no gay culture beyond our genitals to write their novels about, many gay historians can believe in no gay existence before the end of last century.

How can so many of us have lived on this earth for so long and left no history to be written about? We were here! How could we not have been here? Why is it that good historians, like good archaeologists, cannot dig up new old bones?

Why have we found it so difficult to dig up our past? I suspect for the same reason that a psychoanalysis of one's self, to be useful, must be painful. To read how Dutch gay kids were weighted down with rocks and drowned is horrible. To write a history composed mostly of events like this is a depressing undertaking. I suspect there is much less joy than sorrow buried in our graves.

And it is painful for another reason. To know that Abraham Lincoln and Joshua Speed [Lincoln's lifelong friend and political sounding board] were in love with each other for all of their adult lives and that no history book will record this essential truth that could so radically alter how gay people are accepted in this country that worships Lincoln is very painful too. It is one thing, though, to say that Lincoln is gay, which a growing number of us believe, but another to prove it to dissenters. That is the job of historians: finding and proving. It can be done. It took the gay literary world many decades to claim as our own such mainstays of the "straight" literary establishment as [Walt] Whitman, [Willa] Cather, [Thornton] Wilder, [Herman] Melville and, as can be imagined, when you find out that a special friend is just that, it's done us a world of good.

My friend [the playwright] Tony Kushner says it's a confusing time to be gay: "A huge process of redefinition appears to be going on." He calls what we are living through The New Realism, which is certainly better than that silly "postgay" nonsense that one of our more inconsequential publications was trying to float recently.

What's being redefined? The lesbian population is certainly living through a revolution that not many are noticing. Babies, marriages, careers, even an embracing of beauty, as in physically gorgeous, are keynotes here. Are gay men noticing any of this? Gay men only noticed lesbians when they were needed during the plague. Now gay men don't need lesbians anymore. Why, then, would lesbians want to be in a gay movement with gay men now?

My feelings about gay men and the state of our union at present are very complicated because I love gay men and love being gay and hate what we aren't doing so much that I feel estranged, feel sometimes that I'm the only gay man in my world, that I'm not a part of the gay world anymore or the gay movement. I don't recognize anybody. I don't understand what they are saying and doing or not saying and not doing. I speak and understand only one language, and that language seems to have become extinct. I didn't fight all these years to save a world for what I now see happening and not happening.

Why aren't we still afraid of the plague? Why aren't we still fighting to get out of the dark? Why are the few who ask questions like this now called killers ourselves? We want to kill our culture. We want to destroy what gay means. These are mighty accusations. I am not against sex. I am not telling each and everyone, You must live like this and this. I do not believe every gay person should be married, should be monogamous, should not be promiscuous. I am accused of being some puritanical modern Cotton Mather who forbids the joys of the flesh. And here I thought I'd spent all these years just trying to get us a cure so that we could go on living.

But even if I had said one or any of these things, these are not the fights we should be fighting! These aren't what our fights should be about! There are enough awful things happening to each and every gay person in every state in America for us to be terrified of the ceaseless manifestations of the dark hatred from our omnipresent enemies and motivated by it into the same ceaseless defense of our lives. Why can't we see it's still night? Don't we know how little power we have? That's what worries me—that we don't really know. A leader of the Republican party calls us hateful names. He does not do this to Jews. He does not do this to blacks. Why is he allowed to do that to us? And why is it that when he does, when anyone murders us, only a barely visible handful of gay men and lesbians protest? Why aren't we all fighting our enemies instead of each other? Why are we rendered silent by chains not only of the world's making but of our own? We're wrapped up in many of the same selfishnesses that got us into this plague. Yes, I think "barebacking" [having unprotected anal sex] is selfish. Yes, I think Sex Panic! [a New York grassroots organization that advocates sexual freedom and self-determination] is selfish. Yes, I think gay men's exclusion from their sphere of interest of lesbians, and theirs of gay men, is selfish. Yes, I think to define ourselves solely on the basis of our sexualities is selfish.

Something else is selfish. As Tony Kushner says, "The complete disappearance of a concern with political engagement, and the construction of what historical narrative as our academics and intellectuals have constructed into such a hermetically sealed abstract discourse, has helped destroy political activism, has deprived us of the energies of some of our smartest people." Everyone, it often seems, with half a brain has disappeared up his own asshole. Or is taking courses in "queer studies" to learn how to do it.

We still don't even have a name we can all call ourselves. We are many people. We always have been. There is no such thing as a *homosexual* anymore, if there ever was. There is no inclusive word to embrace us all. *Gay* is what we're using now, though I know few who are really happy with this word. *Queer* is truly hateful to many, including me. It is a revolting word and a million miles from connoting pride upon its bearers. It took people of color in America many centuries to coalesce as African-Americans. Perhaps we need more time to locate and agree on our name. Calling ourselves queer and what we study queer is not only an open invitation to alienate our enemies but also to alienate many of us.

"Tell me, is it an honor to forget the dead? Is it in the nature of the living to do that?" Do you know who asked that? Her name is Electra, and she is the star of a 2,500-year-old play by Sophocles that recently sold out in New York City. Electra is one angry young woman. She doesn't want you to forget something she knows is so awful that she wants vengeance. To those who forget, she screams: "Make them suffer, make them weep. . . . May their power turn to nothing. . . . May they die and turn to nothing."

When will gay men and lesbians be able to write plays and novels and histories about our enemies like this? When will we care enough about the murder of our own family, day after day and year after year and century after century, to demand such retribution, repayment, acknowledgment?

It is very hard to become an openly gay person. It is very hard to become a part of the gay movement. It is very hard to become an activist. It is very hard to remain an activist. But I must. Otherwise my world will be taken away from me even more than it already has. Perhaps you think that's not much of a message. But it's the whole world and the only world I can live in, even if I often feel I live in it alone.

Surely the great and ignored theme of our lives is that we are alone. That the isolation I am feeling as a gay man, as a gay activist, as a part of any movement, is the truth of life, not its disguise or its disappointment or its failure.

And in truly being alone, and knowing it, and embracing it, one is never a bystander. The equally great theme of our lives, of our history, of our literature and our art and our culture is responsibility. To ourselves. So that what happens to me happens to you. So that what happens to me might yet happen to you and to us all. So we might know we have loved and honored and remembered each other through the years and since the beginning of time, when we were certainly here. And that many of us died. And that we must never forget.

Our gay ancestors died so that we could be free. You must

think about it in this way. Through their dying we are shown, yet again, that the straight world thinks of us as dispensable, that our enemies, yet again, treat us as worthy of denial and death.

By their dying, it has been, over and over again, our own brothers and sisters who have shown us also this path to freedom, that our gay nation might live: Build thee oh mighty mansions, oh my soul, build thee a new Jerusalem, rage, rage against the dying of the light! They died for us, and we must recall some mighty words inspired by Lincoln himself: It is for us, the living, from these honored dead, to take increased devotion, to be dedicated to the great task remaining before us that we shall not perish from the earth.

"Rage, rage against the dying of the light." [From the poem "Do Not Go Gentle into That Good Night" by Dylan Thomas.]

I will go on raging at the dying of the light.

I ask you to rage with me.

On Being
Black and Gay

JOHN BERNARD JONES

John Bernard Jones is a writer. He is also black and gay. Yet, he notes, "My sexuality is not my primary concern. Nor is my race. Nor is my gender." While he makes it clear that he is not arguing for "staying in the closet," that is, not identifying one's self as gay, he is arguing for choice and respecting each individual's decision whether to come out of that closet.

Jones was inspired to present this argument in response to an article entitled "Black Like You" by Janis Ian, the Grammy-winning singer-songwriter turned journalist and gay activist. In her article, Ian explains how her partner, whom she identifies only as "Mr. Lesbian," confronted a well-known black lesbian singer for not coming out of the closet. In explaining the unfairness of this request, Jones touches on the issues of racism and hypocrisy within the contemporary gay rights movement.

I was riding on the No. 212 bus, reading this big ole gay & lesbian newsmagazine with San Fran mayor Willie Brown on the cover [the March 18, 1997, issue of *The Advocate*] and I got to [musician and writer] Janis Ian's column on page 63. It was called "Black Like You." My eyebrows raised and I thought, Well, it certainly can't be about her. And so it wasn't. It was about a "conversation" between Ms. Ian's sig-nif [significant other], Mr. Lesbian, and some uncredited black woman known only as something like "the well-known songwriting closeted lesbian negress" (aka WKSCLN) or some such. In it, Mr. Lesbian berates WKSCLN about how the latter publicly talks about the trials and tribulations of being black in a racist music industry in particular and society in general, but how WKSCLN remains in the closet about her sexuality in the homophobic music industry in particular and society in general. Despite WKSCLN's "reasons" for remaining closeted, most notably her fear of losing her connectivity to the black community of which she not only is a part but which she claims as her own, Mr. Lesbian proceeds to self-righteously invalidate WKSCLN's concerns all the while Madame Ian apparently wrings her hands in dismay. In short, it took all of about an 800 word column to call WKSCLN nothing less than a hypocrite.

There I was sitting on the bus, literally shaking with dismay. I read the article again to be sure I hadn't misinterpreted the bullshit. Yep. Right there in glorious black 'n' white was the same old hoary Black versus Gay argument, neatly dressed up as a parable. Once again, black gays and lesbian people (you know, the ones like "us") were outright being told that our concerns about being black in a racist society are invalid, that we have an "obligation" to come "out," and that if we don't march down the street with our fists raised high in homo-solidarity with our gay "brothers and sisters," then we are cowards. Cowards! Midway through the column, Mr. Lesbian asks, ". . . why don't black gays come out?" Perhaps I have one answer among many.

A great many black gays don't come out, precisely because of the attitude that Mr. Lesbian and other gays have toward us. The demand that black gays and lesbians realign our concerns, priorities, lifestyles, and lives to fit into the misty-eyed conformity of an ill-defined gay "community" is arrogant condescension at best and racist moral grandstanding at its worst. It is arrogant because it assumes we do not know for ourselves what is or is not good for us on the individual level as issues affect us from day to day.

The demand is racist because it uses a specious argument to assert the superiority of one identity over another. In this case, the argument is to come out. But the question remains, to come out where? Will the gay and lesbian community automatically embrace our songwriter and elevate her to k.d. lang goddesshood on Mr. Lesbian's say-so alone? And the implication that "coming out" will negate the racial indignities and oppressions most people of color must deal with day in and day out is the height of racist absurdity. While I'm at it, let me admit that I assume Mr. Lesbian is not black; how disingenuous of Ms. Ian to not let us know whether or not Mr. Lesbian spoke from a position where she, too, has to deal with the triangularity of identity 'black, gay, & female' as our songwriter must. Mr. Lesbian will not personally make up lost income that our closeted songwriter may lose if she does come out in her industry. Mr. Lesbian cannot replace a mother that could disown her or pay the mortgage on the condo she could lose.

Combating Racism in the Movement

Because Black Gay, Lesbian, Bisexual, and Transgender (GLBT) people have identified HIV/AIDS, hate crime violence, and marriage/domestic partnership as issues of greatest importance, GLBT organizations must address these issues, and the particular ways they affect Black GLBT people, in order to more fully reflect the concerns of all GLBT people.

Discrimination based on race or ethnic identity is a problem for Black GLBT people. The programmatic agendas of all GLBT organizations must include combating discrimination based on race or ethnicity, as well as those systemic concerns—such as class exploitation, sexism, increasing incarceration, inadequate education, and lack of access to quality medical care—which define the lived experience of far too many Black Americans.

Based on the high incidence of experiences of racism in

AN ARGUMENT FOR REASON AND CHOICE

One more thing: I find it curious that a white lesbian making an argument to blacks about owning up to one's "true" identity would refer to her female lover as "Mr." Smacks of a certain kind of hypocrisy in its own right.

I am not making arguments in favor of staying in the closet. What I'm making an argument for is reason and choice. Reason dictates that everyone is not in the same space, place or circumstance that we may be. Choice as a vital component of a diverse community must be respected even if we do not respect the choice itself. In our songwriter's case, the choice is hers as to her status in or out of the closet.

As a black gay man who has never seen the interior of a

interactions with White GLBT people, GLBT communities must address this issue. Dialogue between GLBT Whites and GLBT individuals of color is one component necessary to confront this problem. More fundamentally, the voices, leadership, and inclusion in decision-making of people of color must be a priority for national and local GLBT organizations. There must be a redistribution of power and control in predominately White GLBT organizations to reflect the racial, ethnic, class, and gender diversity of our community.

Those in control of gay community institutions, such as owners and managers of bars and clubs, should examine their practices and make changes to foster more positive interactions among White constituents, Black constituents, and other GLBT people of color. Similar changes should be prioritized and implemented at Gay Pride celebrations throughout the U.S., where many Black GLBT currently feel unwelcome and devalued.

"Say It Loud: I'm Black and I'm Proud: Black Pride Survey 2000," *Policy Institute of the National Gay and Lesbian Task Force.* www.ngltf.org/pi/blackpride.htm.

closet, I am out all the time. I am secure enough in all of my identities that I am myself everywhere I go. But my sexuality is not my primary concern. Nor is my race. Nor is my gender. Sometimes I'm just a writer and other times I'm just a science fiction fan. Each has their turn as circumstances, mood, and priority dictate, sometimes in combination. I don't wear rainbow rings. I don't watch a tv show simply because a gay character is featured or might come out. Sometimes I read gay magazines on crowded buses traveling into the heart of the black community and discreetly cruise a fine brother sitting two seats to the left of me. But I don't ask anyone to read the magazine or for the brother to respond to my attentions. Does this make me a coward, too?

An Activist of the Streets, for the Streets, by the Streets

SYLVIA (RAY) RIVERA

Sylvia (Ray) Rivera often hung out at the Stonewall Inn, a New York City dive bar and disco that was frequented by drag queens and street workers. She did not plan to become an activist. Yet on June 28, 1969, as police herded her and other Stonewall patrons out into the street following a raid, the inn's patrons began to hurl change and other objects at the police and Molotov cocktails at the bar.

The now infamous Stonewall Inn Riot gave birth to a new breed of gay rights activism that was confrontational and unrepentant, and Rivera embraced it.

Following Stonewall, she became involved with both the Gay Liberation Front (GLF) and the Gay Activist Alliance (GAA). In 1970, she cofounded the Street Transvestite Action Revolutionaries (STAR) to provide shelter and support to street kids. Rivera, who died in February 2002 from end-stage liver disease, will always be remembered as a champion of the gay counterculture.

Before gay liberation, if you didn't want someone to bash you, you would look away. You actually looked at the ground. It's like the black person who looks away from the white man. . . . I grew up on the Lower East Side in the Spanish community. That's my heritage. Starting to come out of the closet in my culture, gay people were always belittled and put down. I used to hang out with, and even went out with, a couple of the boys, but in public they would not acknowledge me and I could not acknowledge the fact that we had been to-gether. . . . Learning how to hustle was easy after leaving the neighborhood and going to Forty-second Street, but then I was really dealing with a different kind of straight society. I was used to what my people were saying about me, but dealing with the outside world was completely different. I got into lots of trouble just for looking at straight boys, you know, like say-ing to myself, "Well, this is a beautiful man." Not trying to pick them up or anything, but all of a sudden I'd find a pistol in my face because of the way I walked or the way I acted. . . .

Drag queens and effeminate men never were in a closet. What kills me as a drag queen is that I can go into a gay bar and listen to these so-called macho gay men, "Oh, Mary this, and Miss Thing that." But as soon as I walk into a bar, they know where I'm coming from, and right away I'm shunted aside.

THE STONEWALL INN RAID

Stonewall [Inn in Greenwich Village, New York] was basically a hustlers' bar, not the drag queen bar and not a black bar. It was a hustlers' bar for whites. Only a select few drag queens went there. Mostly you'd get third-world people and drag queens at the Washington Square Bar on Third Street and Broadway. That was one of your big third-world drag-queen bars. . . . The Stonewall was a very nice campy little bar owned by the Mafia—the type of gay bar that was typical of that era. You just went there to party and get high and pop pills and do drugs and drink watered-down drinks. I went to the Stonewall maybe tops ten, fifteen times before it was raided. . . . I was there because we used to make the trip in from Jersey and stop off, have a drink, and then shoot over to the Washington Square Bar. But I'm glad I was there that night [June 28, 1969]. It must have been fate.

I was partying. I was spaced out on black beauties [amphet-amines] and Scotch. We were dancing, my lover and I, and the next thing we know the lights came on, and lights coming on in a gay bar back then meant, "Hey, we're being raided." And, as usual, cops were checking IDs and I started freaking because I didn't think I had my ID, but my lover had his. I had just gotten my draft card, which said I was 4-F, and I was really proud of that. . . . Besides being into drugs, everybody was into politics and into changing the system. My feeling is I was fed up doing and fighting for everybody else. That night I could feel the tension inside and I'm sure everybody else that was there was feeling it, too. It was time for us to get our nook in the people's revolution, to show the world that we are human beings. We were sick and tired of being put down, and things just started happening. . . . It was bad enough that you had to go to these sleazy-ass clubs, but when you had to knock on the door, pay three dollars to get in, get one watered-down drink for the three dollars, and, if you wanted a second watered-down drink, you got it for four bucks. Everybody was just angry. I can only speak for myself, but I felt that I couldn't leave the area until everything was over. I had to see what was going to happen.

RIOT IN THE AFTERMATH

Queens started being filed out, being put into police cars, and the loose change started flying—you know, everybody started throwing it as payoff to the cops. And then the words, the cursing: "Hey, fuck you, pigs. We're not moving. We're tired of this bullshit." You know, all this was happening, and I guess you could taste a bit of freedom before it even happened. Because I know I was feeling good, just for the change being thrown at the cops, for gay brothers and sisters and drag queens and street kids and hustlers just throwing this money at these people like, "You've been treating us like shit all these years? Uh-uh. Now it's our turn!". . . It was one of the greatest moments in my life.

When the first brick and bottles started flying, I'm like, "Oh my God, the revolution is here. Thank God. I'm here and I'm part of it." So I enjoyed being there that night. Every outrageous thing that I did I did out of anger because society had fucked me over for so long. . . . And it was amazing that within ten minutes there were like thousands of gays in the street ready to rebel and fight the police. People were taking a lot of knocks. There was a lot of bloodshed that night. A lot of people got hurt, but people kept coming back. . . . Someone handed me a Molotov cocktail and I had never seen one except on the news about riots. And I'm like, "What am I supposed to do with this?" And this guy said, "Well, I'm gonna light it and you're gonna throw it." And I'm like, "Fine. You light it, I throw it, 'cause if it blows up, I don't want it to blow up on me." It's hard to explain, except that it had to happen one day. . . .

The police knew they were in trouble. They barricaded their asses in there when we started our shit outside, and when they couldn't get backup for forty-five minutes, they were ready to come out shooting. Guns had been drawn. I don't know where the parking meter came from, but we did ram the door open. Molotov cocktails were flying into the bar. Telephone lines somehow mysteriously got cut. You know, through the years no one has figured that out. It's very interesting because Inspector [Seymour] Pine called and asked for backup, and in the middle of his phone call, according to what's been said, the line was cut. And it took forty-five minutes for the Tactical Police Force to get there, and within that forty-five minutes there were so many brothers and sisters out there ready to riot. Traffic had already been stopped, and Molotov cocktails were flying, windows were shattering.

AN ACTIVIST BORN OF THE STREET

For the first four years of the gay liberation movement, [transvestite activist] Lee Brewster put up the money for the bond for the parade. Bebe [Scarpi], another drag queen [and transvestite activist], worked behind the scenes and planned the first four marches. There were a lot of drag queens behind the scenes that could not be seen in front lines. . . . But the drag queens were doing a lot in the background. . . . Well, my dear girlfriend Jean O'Leary, a founder of Radicalesbians, decided that drag queens were insulting to women. In 1973 the 82 Club [in New York] show queens were in the march. Side by side with the Queens Liberation Front banner and the STAR (Street Transvestite Action Revolutionaries) banner. I had been told I was going to speak at the rally. And that's when things just got out of hand. I'm very militant when it comes to certain things, and I didn't appreciate what was going down with Jean O'Leary stating that we were insulting women. There was too much stuff going down that day. Bette Midler was there and Vito Russo [activist and author of *The Celluloid Closet: Homosexuality in the Movies*]—may his soul rest in peace. . . . It was supposed to have been a great march. To this day, I still have people come up to me from the old days and say, "Well, you trashed us on the fourth anniversary." I say, "No, I just stood up for me." . . . Mama Jean and I are still dear friends. She told Vito Russo to kick my ass onstage . . . but I still got up and I spoke my piece. I don't let too many people keep me down. Especially my own. . . .

I'm a very boisterous person, obviously with a temper. Instead of just going up to people and asking them to sign a petition, I would stand in the middle of a block and say, "Excuse me, could you please sign my petition to stop discrimination against homosexuals in housing and in jobs?" And people then would sign any petition. There was a peace rally one night and it was broken up at Forty-second Street and Bryant Park, and the people were pushed down towards Seventh and Eighth Avenues. The Tactical Police Force was out that night, as usual. And I'm standing there doing my thing and the next thing I know: "You're under arrest." I said, "For what?" I said, "I'm not hustling." "Well, you're under arrest." I said, "But for what?" "Well, you can't petition." I said, "But wait a minute, It's in the Constitution that I have the right." I got angry because I know that I'm being arrested for being gay, not because I'm out there soliciting signatures. . . . The first time that I had to appear in court after I was arrested for soliciting the signatures, I had no idea that there were going to be people there to back me up. I walked into this courtroom and all these brothers and sisters that I had never seen and who were all from the Gay Liberation Front (GLF) stood up and applauded.

I said to my friend Josie, who was with me, "Who are all these people and why are they standing up here applauding me?" She says, "Oh, girl, you don't have a lawyer and they're probably gonna throw you in jail and you don't even know it." I said, "Well, if I go to jail, that's fine, too. Who cares?" That's what first turned me on to GLF.

Marsha [P. Johnson] and I always had this dream. When we had STAR House, we tried to make it come true. When Marsha and I got the building on Second Street, the only person that came to help us put that building together was Bob Kohler of GLF. Bebe Scarpi came to do what she could. She would bring us groceries. She would take clothes from her mother's house and things for us to keep for the kids for sleep. . . . I've always known that through the years I have lost my brothers and sisters between drugs and living out on the street. Then I lost Marsha two years ago . . . she had no reason to be out on the streets. She was an icon of the movement. Everybody thinks Sylvia Rivera, but Marsha was higher than me and had no place to live. [Gay rights activist] Randy Wicker took her in. She helped so many people out. Marsha was a frontliner like myself. She was never afraid to take a knock or lay down in front of a police car. Marsha would go out and hustle. She'd be out hustling at night and come in with all the coffee and Danish for the people at STAR House. "All right, girls, I made all this money 'cause, see, this is for our movement." She tried to give all that help when we had STAR House despite all the bad things, including things with me. . . . But I still play little mother hen up there in Westchester [New York] in my apartment. When you come up to my apartment, what do you see? A bunch of drag queens on my floor. They come to me, "Mother Sylvia, do you have something to eat? Can I crash in your house?"

CHRONOLOGY

1915
In speaking to national audiences, birth control advocate Emma Goldman declares homosexuality is not abnormal.

1920
The Amerian Civil Liberties Union (ACLU) is founded; one of their stated goals is the repeal of state sodomy laws.

1924
Influenced by the German gay rights movement, Henry Gerber founds the first American gay rights group—the Society for Human Rights—in Chicago.

1925
After only seven months, Gerber's society is shut down after a member's wife discovers her husband is gay and calls the police, who arrest all members on obscenity charges.

1942
In San Francisco, Jim Kepner begins collecting gay-themed books, building the foundation of what will become the International Gay and Lesbian Archives.

1948
Alfred Kinsey publishes "Sexual Behavior in the Human Male," in which he concludes that 37 percent of American males have had at least one homosexual encounter. In 1953, Kinsey publishes a similar report on women, locating the corresponding statistic at 13 percent.

1950

Harry Hay founds the Mattachine Foundation, the first American gay rights group since Gerber's Society for Human Rights.

1952

Newer Mattachine members—unnerved by accusations that their group is a front for Communist spies—break from the founders, changing their name to the Mattachine Society. Many ousted members eventually join with the emergent organization ONE.

1953

Psychologist Evelyn Hooker publishes a study of the psychological adjustment of gay men, concluding that no psychological difference exists between heterosexual and homosexual men.

1955

Del Martin and Phyllis Lyon found the Daughters of Bilitis, the first American lesbian organization.

1956

James Baldwin publishes *Giovanni's Room*, one of the first mainstream novels to openly discuss gay themes.

1957

Astronomer Franklin Kameny is fired from his job with the U.S. Army because he is gay, transforming Kameny into a lifelong gay rights activist. He becomes the first openly gay congressional candidate in 1971, and is also cofounder of the National Gay Task Force.

1961

Illinois becomes the first state to decriminalize homosexuality.

1963

Bayard Rustin helps Martin Luther King Jr. organize the March on Washington. Rustin, who is open about his homosexuality, is one of the first to suggest that the movements for civil rights and gay rights join forces.

1964

Christopher Isherwood publishes *A Single Man*, which explores a day in the life of a gay man without the misery and isolation that had become characteristic of such novels.

1967

The newspaper *The Advocate* is founded in Los Angeles as a spin-off of a newsletter about police harassment.

1969

The Stonewall Inn, a dive bar and disco in New York City that is a hangout for drag queens and street workers, is raided by police in June. Rioting continues for three days and spawns several new organizations, including the Gay Liberation Front and Gay Activists Alliance. Judy Grahn starts the Women's Press Collective and eventually emerges as a key lesbian theorist.

1970

Bella Abzug and Dianne Feinstein are among the first politicians to seek the gay vote. Abzug serves as cosponsor of the first federal gay rights bill. Transgender activist Sylvia (Ray) Rivera co-founds the Street Transvestite Action Revolutionaries (STAR) to provide shelter and support to street kids.

1971

Journalist and presidential biographer Merle Miller publishes "What It Means to Be a Homosexual" in the *New York Times Magazine*, becoming one of the first major public figures to come out.

1973

The National Gay Task Force (later renamed the National Gay and Lesbian Task Force) is founded. Barbara Grier, her partner Donna McBride, Anyda Marchant, and Muriel Crawford form Naiad Press to publish lesbian literature. Poet Adrienne Rich wins the National Book Award for *Diving into the Wreck*. Lawyer William Thom helps found Lambda Legal Defense Fund, which serves the needs of the gay and lesbian community.

1974

Elaine Noble joins the Massachusetts state legislature, becoming the first openly gay or lesbian politician to be elected to state office. Allan Spear, a Minnesota state senator, comes out. Gay rights activists Barbara Gittings and Franklin Kameny, along with the National Gay Task Force, contribute to the American Psychiatric Association's removal of homosexuality from its list of disorders.

1975

The first gay rights legislation is introduced in Congress. Jonathan Ned Katz publishes *Gay American History*, a groundbreaking publication in gay studies. Leonard Matlovich sues the Air Force after they discharge him for being gay, but he ultimately settles with them after a federal judge orders the Air Force to reinstate him, setting a precedent for future lawsuits.

1976

Joan Nestle, a member of the Gay Activists Alliance, begins the Lesbian Herstory Archives in her New York City apartment. Jean O'Leary, cofounder of the group Lesbian Feminist Liberation, participates in the first meeting of gay activists at the White House.

1977

Harvey Milk wins a seat on the San Francisco board of supervisors, becoming its first openly gay member. He is assassinated the following year, along with Mayor George Moscone, by former supervisor Dan White. Michael Denneny is a founding editor of *Christopher Street*, a gay literary magazine. At St. Martin's Press, he publishes many gay authors, including Randy Shilts, who wrote *And the Band Played On* (1987) about the early days of the AIDS epidemic.

1978
The Briggs initiative, which urges a ban on gay teachers in California, is defeated.

1979
Sister Hysterectoria, Sister Secuba, and the Reverand Mother found the Sisters of Perpetual Indulgence—part street show, part political action—in San Francisco. The Gay and Lesbian Labor Alliance is founded.

1980
The Human Rights Campaign Fund is founded.

1981
Wisconsin passes the first gay rights bill. Adele Starr founds Parents and Friends of Lesbians and Gays (PFLAG). Vito Russo publishes *The Celluloid Closet*, a definitive history of gay issues in movies, and Harvey Fierstein's *Torch Song Trilogy* debuts on Broadway. The first AIDS case surfaces at Memorial Sloan-Kettering Cancer Center in New York City.

1982
The Gay Men's Health Crisis is founded. Michael Hardwick is arrested in his Atlanta home for having sex with another man. The U.S. Supreme Court lets the conviction stand when it upholds Georgia's sodomy law in a 5-4 vote.

1983
Karen Thompson battles for custody of her partner, Sharon Kowalski, who has become a quadriplegic with brain damage

after a car accident. Kowalski's father fights Thompson, prohibiting her from visiting his daughter. Thompson is eventually named Kowalski's legal guardian in 1991.

1985

Activist Cleve Jones develops the concept of the AIDS quilt, which is launched two years later as the Names Project. Actor Rock Hudson dies from AIDS complications, bringing the disease into the national spotlight. The Gay and Lesbian Alliance Against Defamation (GLAAD) is founded.

1987

Randy Shilts publishes *And the Band Played On*, his account of the political apathy that contributed to the spread of AIDS. Larry Kramer inspires the creation of a more direct action group, the AIDS Coalition to Unleash Power (ACT UP).

1989

Leslea Newman's *Heather Has Two Mommies*, a book about lesbian parenting, and Michael Willhoite's *Daddy's Roommate* are published. Marshall Kirk and Hunter Madsen publish *After the Ball: How America Will Conquer Its Fear and Hatred of Gays in the '90s*, an analysis of the contemporary gay rights movement.

1990

Mandy Carter urges North Carolina gay and lesbian voters to go against incumbent Republican senator Jesse Helms. Though unsuccessful, she eventually becomes field program consultant for the Black Gay and Lesbian Leadership Forum.

1991

Historian Martin Duberman founds the Center for Lesbian and Gay Studies at the City University of New York.

1992

Paul Monette wins the National Book Award for *Becoming a Man: Half a Life Story*, and his works are celebrated as some of the most moving records of the AIDS epidemic. Bob Hattoy, an openly gay political consultant with AIDS, is appointed assistant White House personnel director.

1993

Roberta Achtenberg, a San Francisco supervisor, is appointed assistant secretary of Housing and Urban Development, making her the highest-ranking openly gay person to serve in an administration. After dropping out of school in Ashland, Wisconsin, Jamie Nabozny sues the district for not ending his classmates' mental and physical abuse of him because he is gay. In 1996, he is awarded $900,000 after a federal jury rules that administrators intentionally discriminated against him.

1995

Gays and lesbians are no longer automatically denied U.S. government security clearances.

1996

Co-counsels Dan Foley and Evan Wolfson win a landmark court case that makes Hawaii the first state to not ban gays and lesbians from marrying. The citizens of Hawaii later amend their state constitution to define a legal marriage as a union between one man and one woman only, effectively overturning the decision.

1997

Jon and Michael Galluccio of Maywood, New Jersey, win a landmark case from the state's supreme court, which allows them to jointly adopt. They now have three children. Editors Mark Blasius and Shane Phelan publish *We Are Everywhere: A Historical Sourcebook of Gay and Lesbian Politics.*

1998

Tammy Baldwin becomes the first openly gay representative to win a first-time election to Congress. The Boy Scouts of America oust leader James Dale when they discover he is gay. In 2000, the U.S. Supreme Court in a 5–4 decision sided with the Scouts. Writing for the majority, Chief Justice Rehnquist said that forcing the Scouts to rehire Dale "would significantly burden the organization's [First Amendment] right to oppose or disfavor homosexual conduct." Matthew Shepard dies in what begins as a robbery but ends when he is beaten for being gay. To bring meaning to her son's death, his mother, Judy, becomes a gay rights activist.

2000

Vermont passes the Civil Union Law, which provides same-sex couples with the same rights, privileges, and responsibilities as heterosexual married couples, including dependent health insurance coverage, hospital visitation, emergency care decisions, estate inheritance, and social security survivor benefits. President Bill Clinton declares June Gay and Lesbian Pride Month. A New Jersey court grants visitation rights to a lesbian woman who helped raise her former partner's twins for the first two years of their lives, and a New York judge grants another lesbian woman permanent visitation rights to see the two children she helped raise.

2001

Twenty-six states along with the District of Columbia now prohibit discrimination based on sexual orientation, and four states along with the District of Columbia also prohibit discrimination based on gender identity. Connecticut becomes the first state to pass a law allowing second-parent adoption.

2002

The Pennsylvania Legislature passes a bill by a vote of 118–79 to extend the state's hate crime laws to include actual or perceived sexual orientation, gender, and gender identity. Several more states pass laws prohibiting discrimination based on gender identity. The U.S. Supreme Court agrees to hear a case concerning the states' antisodomy laws to consider whether these laws are an unconstitutional invasion of privacy. Four states—Texas, Oklahoma, Kansas, and Missouri—currently have antisodomy laws while eleven other states have laws that outlaw some form of both heterosexual and homosexual activity.

FOR FURTHER RESEARCH

Books

Bruce Bawer, *Beyond Queer: Challenging Gay Left Orthodoxy.* New York: Free Press, 1996.

Allida M. Black, ed., *Modern American Queer History.* Philadelphia: Temple University Press, 2001.

Mark Blasius and Shane Phelan, eds., *We Are Everywhere: A Historical Sourcebook of Gay and Lesbian Politics.* New York: Routledge, 1997.

Eric Brandt, ed., *Dangerous Liaisons: Blacks and Gays and the Struggle for Equality.* New York: New Press, 1999.

Chris Bull, ed., *Come Out Fighting: A Century of Essential Writing on Gay and Lesbian Liberation.* New York: Thunder's Mouth Press/Nation Books, 2001.

Chris Bull and John Gallagher, eds., *Perfect Enemies: The Battle Between the Religious Right and the Gay Movement.* Lanham, MD: Madison Books, 2001.

Charlotte Bunch and Nancy Myron, eds., *Class and Feminism: A Collection of Essays from the Furies.* Baltimore: Diana, 1974.

Thomas C. Caramagno, *Irreconcilable Differences?: Intellectual Stalemate in the Gay Rights Debate.* Westport, CT: Praeger, 2002.

David Deitcher, ed., *The Question of Equality: Lesbian and Gay Politics in America Since Stonewall.* New York: Scribner, 1995.

John D'Emilio, William B. Turner, and Urvashi Vaid, eds., *Creating Change: Sexuality, Public Policy, and Civil Rights.* New York: St. Martin's Press, 2000.

Michael Denneny, Charles Ortleb, and Thomas Steele, eds., *The Christopher Street Reader*. New York: Perigree Books, 1983.

David M. Donahue, *Lesbian, Gay, Bisexual, and Transgender Rights: A Human Rights Perspective*. Minneapolis: University of Minnesota, 2000.

Martin Duberman, *About Time: Exploring the Gay Past*. New York: Meridian, 1991.

Richard Goldstein, *The Attack Queers: Liberal Society and the Gay Right*. London: Verso, 2002.

Harry Hay, *Radically Gay: Gay Liberation in the Words of Its Founder*. Boston: Beacon Press, 1996.

Loraine Hutchins and Lani Kaahumanu, eds., *Bi Any Other Name: Bisexual People Speak Out*. Boston: Alyson Publications, 1991.

Karla Jay and Allen Young, *Out of the Closets: Voices of Gay Liberation*. New York: Douglas, 1972.

Marshall Kirk and Hunter Madsen, *After the Ball: How America Will Conquer Its Fear and Hatred of Gays in the '90s*. New York: Doubleday, 1989.

Larry Kramer, *Reports from the Holocaust: The Making of an AIDS Activist*. New York: St. Martin's Press, 1989.

Audre Lorde, *Sister Outsider: Essays and Speeches*. Trumansburg, NY: Crossing Press, 1984.

Robert B. Marks Ridinger, *The Gay and Lesbian Movement: References and Resources*. New York: G.K. Hall, 1996.

Craig A. Rimmerman, *From Identity to Politics: The Lesbian and Gay Movements in the United States*. Philadelphia: Temple University Press, 2002.

Vincent J. Samar, ed., *The Gay Rights Movement*. Chicago: Fitzroy Dearborn, 2001.

Randy Shilts, *And the Band Played On: Politics, People, and the AIDS Epidemic.* New York: St. Martin's Press, 1987.

Randy Shilts, ed., *The Mayor of Castro Street: The Life and Times of Harvey Milk.* New York: St. Martin's Press, 1982.

Mark Thompson, ed., *Long Road to Freedom: The Advocate History of the Gay and Lesbian Movement (Stonewall Inn Editions).* New York: St. Martin's Press, 1994.

Carla Trujillo, *Chicana Lesbians: The Girls Our Mothers Warned Us About.* Berkeley: Third Woman Press, 1991.

Carole S. Vance, ed., *Pleasure and Danger: Exploring Female Sexuality.* London: Pandora Press, 1992.

Films

After Stonewall. Dir. Great Schiller. First Run Features, 1999.

All God's Children. Dirs. Dr. Dee Mosbacher, Francis Reid, and Dr. Sylvia Rhue. Woman Vision, National Black Gay and Lesbian Leadership Forum, and National Gay and Lesbian Task Force, 1996.

And the Band Played On. Dir. Roger Spottiswoode. HBO Pictures, 1993.

Before Stonewall: The Making of a Gay and Lesbian Community. Dir. Greta Schiller. First Run Features, 1984.

The Celluloid Closet. Dirs. Rob Epstein and Jeffrey Friedman. Columbia TriStar, 1996.

March in April. Dir. Stephen Kinsella. First Run Features, 1993.

Out of the Past: The Struggle for Gay and Lesbian Rights in America. Dir. Jeff Dupree. A-Pix Entertainment, Inc., 1997.

The Times of Harvey Milk. Dir. Robert Epstein. Image Entertainment, 1988.

Internet Sources

Juan Battle et al., "Say It Loud: I'm Black and I'm Proud: Black Pride Survey 2000," *Policy Institute of the National Gay and Lesbian Task Force.* www.ngltf.org.

Paula Ettelbrick, "Stabilizing Family Through Civil Union Laws," *National Gay and Lesbian Task Force: Library and Publications*, June 19, 2000. www.ngltf.org.

John Bernard Jones, "Black Like Me," *Blackstripe*, March 21, 1999. www. blackstripe.com.

Larry Kramer, "Yesterday, Today, and Tomorrow," *Advocate*, March 1999. www.advocate.com.

Robert N. Minor, "The Legend of the Stonewall Inn: What Does It Mean?" *Gay Today*, June 17, 2002. www.gaytoday. com.

Jack Nichols, "Remembering the Stonewall Era," *Gay Today*, June 14, 1999. www.gaytoday.com.

Gregory J. Rosmaita, "The Forgotten Populist, Harvey Milk," 1995. www.hicom.net.

Riki Wilchins, "In Memory of Stonewall Warrior Sylvia Rivera: A Woman for Her Time," *Village Voice*, February 27–March 5, 2002. www.villagevoice.com.

Periodicals

James Baldwin, "Preservation of Innocence," *Zero*, vol. 1, no. 2, 1949.

Richard Berkowitz, Michael Callen, and Richard Dworkin, "We Know Who We Are: Two Gay Men Declare War on Promiscuity," *New York Native*, November 1982.

Anita Cornwell, "From a Soul Sister's Notebook," *Ladder*, 1972.

Steven Dansky, John Knoebel, and Kenneth Pitchford, "The Effeminist Manifesto," *Double-F: A Magazine of Effeminism*, 1973.

Leo Ebreo, "A Homosexual Ghetto?" *Ladder*, 1965.

John Gallagher, "Are We Really Asking for Special Rights? Gay Rights Opponents Have Found an Argument That Plays Well to Most Americans," *Advocate*, April 14, 1998.

————, "Take a Wilde Ride: From Oscar Wilde to the Rev. Jimmy Creech, a Selective History of Gay and Lesbian Activism," *Advocate*, August 17, 1999.

————, "The Transgender Revolution," *Advocate*, December 10, 1996.

Ted Gideonse et al., "Our Best and Brightest Activists," *Advocate*, August 17, 1999.

Daniel Harris, "The Death of Camp: Gay Men and Hollywood Diva Worship, from Reverence to Ridicule," *Salmagundi*, Fall 1996.

Arnie Kantrowitz, "Letter to the Queer Generation," *NYQ*, 1992.

Del Martin, "If That's All There Is," *Ladder*, 1970.

Tammy A. Richardson, Nathalie Rayes, and Jerome Rabow, "Homophobia and the Denial of Human Rights," *Transformations*, March 31, 1998.

Jeffrey Schmalz, "Whatever Happened to AIDS?" *New York Times Magazine*, November 28, 1993.

Walt Shepperd, "AIDS at 20: More Education and Money Are Needed to Dispel the Myths That Accompany the Deadly Disease," *Syracuse New Times*, December 5, 2001.

Richard Tate, "The Battle to Be a Parent: Recognizing the Rights of Gay and Lesbian Parents Is the Latest Frontier for Equality," *Advocate*, January 30, 2001.

Shirley Willer, "What Concrete Steps Can Be Taken to Further the Homophile Movement?" *Ladder*, 1966.

Jeff Winters, "A Frank Look at the Mattachine: Can Homosexuals Organize?" *ONE Magazine*, 1954.

Websites

ACT UP, www.actupny.org. Founded by activist Larry Kramer in 1987, ACT UP—the AIDS Coalition to Unleash Power—is a direct action group that is committed to ending the AIDS crisis.

AIDS and HIV History, www.avert.org. This repository of first-hand materials, photographs, and other information is part of AVERT, an international HIV and AIDS charity based in the United Kingdom.

AIDS Memorial Quilt, www.aidsquilt.org. The quilt, begun in 1987, is a memorial in progress and the largest community arts project in the world. Each panel in the quilt commemorates the life of a person lost to AIDS. To date, there are more than forty-four thousand panels.

Bisexual Foundation, www.bisexual.org. This site provides information and resources for the bisexual community.

Blackstripe, www.blackstripe.com. This site provides information and resources for gay, lesbian, bisexual, and transgendered people of African descent.

Committee on Lesbian and Gay History, www.usc.edu/isd/archives/clgh/. This committee is an affiliated society of the American Historical Association. Founded in 1979, it promotes the study of homosexuality through the development of specialized courses, local history archives, and scholarly conferences.

Gay and Lesbian Alliance Against Defamation (GLAAD), www.glaad.org. GLAAD ensures accurate and inclusive representation of all individuals and events in all media in order to combat discrimination based on gender identity and sexual orientation.

Gay and Lesbian Historical Society, www.glhs.org. This society, which merged with the International Museum of Gay and Lesbian History in 2002, maintains one of the world's largest collections of primary source material about gay, lesbian, bisexual, and transgender history.

Gay History, www.gayhistory.com. This site, an ongoing project, provides an introduction to the stories and people of modern gay history.

Gay Men's Health Crisis (GMHC), www.gmhc.org. Begun in 1982, GMHC is a nonprofit community organization committed to national leadership in the fight against AIDS.

Gender Public Advocacy Coalition (GenderPAC), www.gpac. org. To end discrimination and violence caused by gender stereotypes, GenderPAC works to change public attitudes, educate elected officials, and secure legal rights.

Gerber Hart Library, www.gerberhart.org. The library was established in 1981 as a records archive for the gay, lesbian, bisexual, and transgendered communities in the United States, and it is the largest of its kind in the Midwest.

Human Rights Campaign (HRC), www.hrc.org. Founded in 1980, the HRC today is one of America's largest gay and lesbian organizations, effectively lobbying Congress, mobilizing grassroots action committees, and increasing public awareness to secure the civil rights of those in the gay, lesbian, bisexual, and transgender communities.

Lesbian Herstory Project, www.lib.usc.edu/~retter/main. html. This site provides an online record of lesbian history and contains information on lesbian accomplishments and contributions, relevant journals and archives, and scholarly projects.

The National Archive of Gay and Lesbian History, www. gaycenter.org/archives. Founded in 1990, the archive houses thousands of papers, periodicals, correspondence and photographs from the gay, lesbian, bisexual, and transgender communities. These materials are made accessible to the public through regular exhibits, publications, and scholarly research activities.

The National Coalition for Gay, Lesbian, and Bisexual Youth, www.outproud.org. This site provides information and resources for gay, lesbian, bisexual, and transgendered youth.

National Gay and Lesbian Task Force, www.ngltf.org. Founded in 1973, this national organization works to ensure the civil rights of gay, lesbian, bisexual, and transgendered people. They believe in the need for a powerful political movement, supported at the local level by community leaders.

National Transgender Advocacy Coalition, www.ntac.org. This coalition works to reform legal and societal attitudes toward the transgendered and other gender diverse individuals.

ONE Institute and Archives, oneinstitute.org. This site describes ONE's archival materials regarding the gay, lesbian, bisexual, and transgendered communities.

Out of the Past: 400 Years of Lesbian and Gay History in America, www.pbs.org/outofthepast. This is the companion site to the PBS documentary *Out of the Past*, which touches on nearly four hundred years of lesbian and gay history and allows users to share their own news and stories.

Parents, Families, and Friends of Lesbians and Gays (PFLAG), www.pflag.org. Through advocacy and education, this national, nonprofit organization provides a forum in which to discuss sexual orientation and gender identity. PFLAG currently boasts over 460 affiliates, totaling more than eighty thousand members.

Partners Task Force for Gay and Lesbian Couples, www. buddybuddy.com. This site supports gay and lesbian couples by offering more than two hundred articles and other resources about such topics as domestic partner benefits, relationship tips, and parenting.

People with a History: An Online Guide to Lesbian, Gay, Bisexual, and Trans* History, www.fordham.edu/halsall/pwh. This site houses hundreds of original texts, discussions, and images from all regions of the world, moving from the ancient Mediterranean era to the twenty-first century.

Queer Resources Directory, www.qrd.org. This directory contains over twenty-five thousand files, including news stories, first-hand documents, and hyperlinks about issues concerning the gay, lesbian, bisexual, and transgender communities.

Sisters of Perpetual Indulgence, www.thesisters.org. Since 1979, the Sisters—part street show, part political action committee—have raised awareness as well as money for many gay causes. Though founded in San Francisco, the Sisters now have orders in six countries.

INDEX

Adler, Alfred, 38
advertising
  antigay, 99–100
  changing beliefs through, 101
  creating appealing stereotypes through, 100, 102
  power of pictures and, 103
African Americans
  choosing to not come out, 186–90
  combating racism of, 188, 189
  frustration with gay rights movement by, 16
  parallel struggle with gay rights and Jewish struggle and, 50, 54
AIDS (acquired immune deficiency syndrome)
  bisexuals and, 146–47
  denial of drug treatment for, 107–109
  gains in fighting, 178
  in gay community
    must mobilize protests on, 113–14
    passivity on, 112–13
    responsibility to each other and, 105–106, 114–15, 184–85
    uniting to fight, 111–12
  honoring the dead from, 180
  influence on gay rights

movement, 18–19, 179
physicians/hospitals for, 106–107
public perception of, 18
as a threat to the existence of gay men, 104–105
treatment delays for, 109–10
wasted money on, 110
AIDS Action Council, 159
Alioto, Joseph L., 164
Allen, Woody, 115
American Foundation for AIDS Research, 115
American Psychiatric Association, 19–20
Ampligen, 108
artists, 37
attire, 139–41
AZT, 108–10

Baldwin, James, 40
Baroni, Geno, 122
Beatty, Warren, 115
Bernstein, Leonard, 115
bisexuals
  challenges of, 146–52
  gains made by, 145–46
  myths and truths on, 150, 151
  strategies for liberation of, 152–57
  women's liberation and, 152
Blasius, Mark, 52, 53
Brewster, Lee, 194
Bryant, Anita, 169

contradictions in
persecution of, 28–30
as criminals or of lower
class, 30–32
deviance of, vs. heterosexual
deviance, 38
discrimination of vs. lifestyle
of, as creating neuroses of,
26–27
ghettoization and isolation
of, 54–55, 90–91, 184
history of persecution of,
24–25
lack of histories written on,
180–81
name for, 13, 183–84
need for political leadership
by, 171–74
redefining, 181–82
shattering invisibility of,
83–84
see also AIDS; butch-fems;
homosexuality; lesbians
Gay Women's Liberation, 165
gender
differences and roles, 43–44
drudgery tasks and
childcare and, 78
in gay rights movement,
57–59
stereotypes, 44–46
GenderPAC (Public
Advocacy Coalition), 21
Gentlemen's Agreement
(Hobson), 47
Gerber, Henry, 14, 24
God, 42–43
Grabowski, Henry, 108
Gramick, Jeannine, 116–19,
122, 123

gynarchism, 72

Hall, Radclyffe, 143
Hawaii, 20
Hay, Harry, 14
Heather Has Two Mommies
(Newman), 20
heterosexuality
butch-fem relationships and,
135, 139
conservatives hindering gay
community unification
with, 64–65
deviance of, vs. homosexual
deviance, 38
Hewman, Leslie, 20
Hobson, Laura Keane Z., 47
homophile organizations. *See*
organizations
homophile publications,
164–65
homosexuality
as caused by both nature and
environment, 35
"cure" for, 27–28, 31
is not a neurosis, 38–39
as a neurosis, 25–26
prejudiced propaganda on,
32–34
shades and degrees of, 37
social factors in making,
34–35
social value of, 35–37
as "unnatural," 40–42
see also gays and lesbians
homosexuals. *See* gays and
lesbians
hospitals, 106–107
Huhner, Max, 35
Human Rights Campaign

Fund (HRCF), 158
Hume, David, 95

ICN Pharmaceuticals, 109
Institute for Immunological
Disorders, 106, 107
insurance policies, 107

Jastrow, Otto, 39
Jenkins, Walter, 51
Jews, 49–54
Johnson, Marsha P., 196
Jones, John Bernard, 186

Kirk, Marshall, 13, 99, 158
Knoebel, John, 71
Koch, Ed, 110–11
Koertge, Noretta, 92
Kohler, Bob, 196
Koop, C. Everett, 115
Kowalski, Sharon, 129–30
Kramer, Larry, 13, 19, 104,
175–78
Kushner, Tony, 181–82, 183

Lake Snell Perry and
Associates, 129, 131
Lambda Legal Defense and
Education Fund, 158
Lavender Hill Mob, 113
legislation
on gays and lesbians in
government employment,
20
on heterosexual vs.
homosexual acts, 32
on natural cravings, 29–30
see also Civil Union Law
Lesbian Herstory Archives,
141

lesbians
Catholic nuns as, 121–22,
123–24
first organization of, 15–16
gay men giving notice to,
182
joining in common cause of
male sexuality, 59
name for, 13
problems of, vs. problems of
gay men, 58
suggestions to gay rights
community for unity
within, 60–61
see also butch-fems; gays and
lesbians
Levi, Jeff, 159
Lincoln, Abraham, 181
literature, 44–46, 143, 184
Loughery, John, 66–67
Lyon, Phyllis, 15

Madsen, Hunter, 13, 99, 158
Mansell, Peter, 107, 109–10
marriage
same-sex, 20
as a way to "cure"
homosexuality, 27–28
see also Civil Union Law
Martin, Del, 15, 162
masculinity, 74–76
masochism, 76
masturbation, 35
Mattachine Society, 14–15,
52, 53
Maxwell, William, 46–47
May, Sister Ruth Marie, 121
media
on AIDS, 18
lobbying in, 20

men
  literature stereotypes of,
    44–45
  principles of effeminate,
    72–78
  see also AIDS; gays and
    lesbians; gender
Mendanhall, George, 164
Midler, Bette, 195
Milk, Harvey, 20, 168
  as forgotten, 80
  as free of party of politics,
    85
  on inner-city problems,
    86–88
  mobilization of gay
    community's political
    power by, 84–85
  political goals of, 81–84
ministry, Catholic. See New
  Ways Ministry
Morgan, Robin, 163
Moynihan, Patrick, 110–11

National Assembly of
  Religious Brothers, 122–23
National Coalition of
  American Nuns, 122–23
National Coalition of Black
  Lesbians and Gays, 159
National Gay and Lesbian
  Task Force (NGLTF),
    19–20, 158
National Gay Rights
  Advocates, 158
National Institutes of Health
  (NIH), 110, 120
nature
  God and, 42–43
  vs. nurture, 34–35

relationship between men
  and women and, 40, 43–44
vs. "unnatural," 40–42
Nestle, Joan, 134
neuroses, 25–27, 38–39
Newman, Leslea, 20
New Ways Ministry
  accomplishments of, 122–23
  function of, 117
  gay nuns' retreat and, 120–21
  obstacles of, 119–20
  as safe haven for gay
    religious, 117–19
  support for, 118–19
New York Post (newspaper), 20
Nichols, Jack, 63
North American Conference
  on Homophile
  Organizations (NACHO),
    162–63, 165
Nugent, Robert, 116–18,
    121–22

O'Leary, Jean, 194, 195
ONE, 15
organizations
  at beginning of gay rights
    movement, 14–16
  bisexual, 145, 153–56
  Catholic, 122–23
  combating racism in, 188,
    189
  fear of joining, 55
  first lesbian, 57
  following Stonewall Inn
    riot, 17–18
  gay men's, as excluding
    women, 163–64
  goal of integration of, 54,
    55–56

must mobilize protests on
fight against AIDS, 113–14
need for centralized, 158–60

Parisex, 24
partners, same-sex
rights for
need for, 129–30
public support for, 129, 131
see also Civil Union Law
patriarchy, 72
pharmaceutical companies,
108–109
Phelan, Shane, 22, 52, 53
physicians, 106–107
Pitchford, Kenneth, 71
political action committees
(PACs), 80–81
politics, gay
allies for, 92–93
American principles and, 92
conservatives are not gaining
upper hand in, 169–71
demands of, 91
enemies in, 93–94
gay culture is necessary for,
91
lack of concern for, 183
must give people hope,
172–74
need for gay leadership in,
171–72
power and, 94–96
see also gay rights movement;
Milk, Harvey
Popham, Paul, 111–12, 113
Praxis Pharmaceuticals, 109
prostitution, 36
psychoanalysis, 25–26, 39

"queer," 183–84
Queer Nasty (online
magazine), 21
Quixote Center, 118

racism, 187–88, 189
Reagan, Ronald, 115
research, 110
Reverend Mother, 17–18
ribavirin, 108–109
Rivera, Sylvia (Ray), 191
Rosmaita, Gregory J., 79
Russo, Vito, 195

sado-masculinity, 74–76
Salvatorians, 118
same-sex marriage. *See* Civil
Union Law; marriage, same-
sex
San Francisco
city employees in, 88
ethnic neighborhoods in, 81,
84
Harvey Milk's political goals
for, 86–88
legacy of, 88–89
political action committees
in, 80–81
prior to Harvey Milk's
arrival, 80
urban renewal in, 85–86
Scarpi, Bebe, 194, 196
Serenade (Cain), 45–46
sexism, 72
Shepard, Matthew, 178
Shilts, Randy, 115
Shuster, Rebecca, 21, 145
Sister Hysterectoria, 17–18
Sister Secuba, 17–18
Sisters of Perpetual